# LOST LINES
# Railway Treasures

LOST LINES
# Railway Treasures

Nigel Welbourn

crecy.co.uk

First published 2018

© Nigel Welbourn 2018

ISBN 9780860936916

Printed in Bulgaria by Multiprint

**Crécy Publishing Ltd**
1a Ringway Trading Estate, Shadowmoss Rd,
Manchester M22 5LH
**www.crecy.co.uk**

*Front cover:* Cahersiveen Viaduct, May 2005. *Author*

*Rear cover:* Meldon Viaduct, July 2016. *Author*
*Top inset:* Crystal Palace subway, May 1995. *Author*
*Bottom inset:* Strathpeffer station, June 2010. *Author*

**Picture credits**
Every effort has been made to identify and correctly attribute photographic credits. Should any error have occurred this is entirely unintentional.

# Contents

# Abbreviations

| | | | |
|---|---|---|---|
| BCDR | Belfast & County Down Railway | LMS | London, Midland & Scottish Railway |
| BNCR | Belfast & Northern Counties Railway | LNER | London & North Eastern Railway |
| BM | Brecon & Merthyr Railway | LNWR | London & North Western Railway |
| BR | British Railways | LSWR | London & South Western Railway |
| BTH | British Transport Hotels | LTSR | London, Tilbury & Southend Railway |
| CR | Caledonian Railway | LT | London Transport |
| CLC | Cheshire Lines Committee | L&B | Lynton & Barnstaple Railway |
| CDR | County Donegal Railways | M&GN | Midland & Great Northern Joint Railway |
| CIÉ | Córas Iompair Éireann | MR | Midland Railway |
| DEMU | Diesel Electric Multiple Unit | M&SW | Midland & South Western Junction Railway |
| DMU | Diesel Multiple Unit | MSLR | Mid-Suffolk Light Railway |
| ECML | East Coast Main Line | NCB | National Coal Board |
| GSWR | Glasgow & South Western Railway | NCC | Northern Counties Committee |
| GCR | Great Central Railway | NRM | National Railway Museum |
| GER | Great Eastern Railway | NSR | North Staffordshire Railway |
| GNR | Great Northern Railway | NSJ | Norfolk & Suffolk Joint Railway |
| GNR(I) | Great Northern Railway of Ireland | NBR | North British Railway |
| GNSR | Great North of Scotland Railway | NER | North Eastern Railway |
| GSR | Great Southern Railways | PLA | Port of London Authority |
| GWR | Great Western Railway | S&D | Somerset & Dorset Joint Railway |
| HR | Highland Railway | SECR | South Eastern & Chatham Railway |
| HB | Hull & Barnsley Railway | SER | South Eastern Railway |
| LYR | Lancashire & Yorkshire Railway | SR | Southern Railway |
| LOR | Liverpool Overhead Railway | UTA | Ulster Transport Authority |
| LBSCR | London, Brighton & South Coast Railway | WR | Western Region |
| LMR | London Midland Region | | |

# Introduction

Those aware of Nigel Welbourn's long-running and critically acclaimed 'Lost Lines' series will know that the 15 volumes cover over 400 lost lines. Illustrated with black and white photographs, the individual books embrace specific areas and regions of the British Isles. This book by the same author takes a slightly different perspective, by taking an overview of Britain and selecting some of the best loved lost lines, together with the most interesting closed railway remains, and illustrating these in full colour.

The book also uniquely weaves a history of Britain's railways through lost lines and their surviving treasures. Starting with early passenger closures dating back to the 1820s, more losses came with World War 1 and in the economic depression of the late 1920s and early 1930s. World War 2 saw a spate of further closures.

None of the previous loses were to surpass the savage cuts by British Railways in the 1960s instigated by the infamous Beeching Report, named after the BR Chairman at that time. Closures came to a near end in the 1970s, but losses of the Woodhead, Spalding–March and Tunbridge Wells West lines in the 1980s, the Aldwych and Ongar branches and Dover Western Docks in the 1990s, together with the Folkestone Harbour branch in 2014, continued a never-ending trend.

The journey between the first closures up to the present day looks at a fascinating variety of lost lines and railway subjects. The book includes references to the largest and smallest closed stations and from the largest lost remains to intriguing tiny relics. In this context, the author has selected his favourite top 10 surviving lost lines treasures. The author also selects his own 10 key closed lines in three categories: main lines, scenic lines and those with the best prospect of re-opening.

Having visited every major lost line in the country from the remotest rural area to the heart of great cities, over a period in excess of 50 years, this widely-researched book provides a wealth of information.

In view of their close links to Britain the island of Ireland and the Isle of Man are also included in this book and clearly have a number of their own treasures.

Dunston Staithes, on the River Tyne outside Newcastle, were built to transfer coal to seagoing colliers. They were opened by the NER in 1893 and extensions were completed by 1903. In some years, over 5 million tonnes of coal were dispatched, before closure came in 1980. The timber pier is the largest in Europe and part is seen here in September 2016. *Author*

# 1

# Early closures

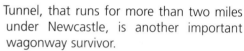

Horse-drawn wagonways, also known as tramroads, developed particularly where there was coal and can be traced back to the 1600s. The Causey Arch in Durham was built in 1725–6 and at the time was the largest single-span stone bridge in Britain. It was built for a branch of the Tanfield Wagonway, one of a number of wagonways that transported coal to the River Tyne. The wooden tracks were out of use by the beginning of the 19th century, but the bridge survived and is the wagonway era's greatest treasure. The nearby Victoria Tunnel, that runs for more than two miles under Newcastle, is another important wagonway survivor.

The massive growth of the Industrial Revolution needed ever better transport and wagonways were gradually converted into, or replaced by, railways. An example was the Middleton Railway, authorised by an Act of Parliament in 1758 and linking Leeds to the nearby coalfield. Horses were eventually replaced by steam power, wooden tracks by iron rails, whilst a new section replaced a steeply graded part of the original route.

In Wales, the discovery that iron could be smelted with coal was to utterly change the landscape and society of many of the green valleys of South Wales. On the Merthyr Tramroad in 1804, a locomotive built by Richard Trevithick at the Penydarren Ironworks, successfully hauled a train loaded with 10 tonnes of bar iron for almost 10 miles, settling a wager as to the usefulness of steam traction between two iron masters. The Merthyr Tramroad began to fall out of use when the adjoining standard-gauge railway network was expanded in the 1850s.

The Oystermouth Railway, on the shores of Swansea Bay, opened to passengers in March 1807, becoming the first railway to do so. The horse-drawn service ceased in 1827, due to competition from horse buses on the adjoining road. It thus became the first length of passenger railway to close due to road competition. By 1860, after a period of dereliction, the track was reinstated and passenger services resumed.

The Belvoir Castle horse-drawn line ran from the Grantham Canal to the castle, opening in 1814. Coal was conveyed into the castle and a branch ran to the kitchens to supply provisions. The line fell out of regular use in 1918 and was mostly dismantled during World War 2. However, remains of the oldest cast iron 'I'-shaped track still *in situ* in the castle grounds are seen here in July 2000. *Kind permission of His Grace the Duke of Rutland*

*Right:* The Stockton & Darlington Railway was the first public railway to use steam from the beginning. At Stockton, the weigh house, dating from 1825, is the oldest surviving building and is seen, looking in design rather like a road toll house, in November 1996. The original inclines on the route at Etherley and Brusselton were closed to remaining traffic in 1858. *Author*

*Below right:* The Merthyr Tramroad, also known as the Penydarren Tramroad, began to fall out of use in the 1850s and was abandoned, or rebuilt as a railway, by 1890. A high-arched over bridge, that would have accommodated a tall locomotive chimney, is seen at Pontygwaith, north of Quaker's Yard, in February 2004. Two centuries earlier, a steam engine hauled a freight train between Merthyr Tydfil and Abercynon. The rest, as they say, is history. *Author*

*Below:* The slate industry in North Wales spawned a huge network of narrow-gauge lines. A slate wagon from the Nantle quarry, dating from 1828, is preserved at Tywyn in June 1999. The double-flanged wheels were capable of sliding along their axles in order to run on roughly-gauged track. Eight slate quarries closed in North Wales between 1908 and 1913 marking the start of a long decline. *Author*

The original small Hampton station, dating from 1839, was built by the Birmingham & Derby Railway. As the railway network expanded, it was replaced by a nearby larger station in 1884 and this was renamed Hampton-in-Arden in 1886. A freight siding to the original station survived until 1952, whilst the building remained in July 2001. *Author*

Although the Industrial Revolution did not influence southern England to the same extent as the north, as there were fewer minerals, the Surrey Iron Railway opened in 1803. Running from the River Thames to near Croydon, it used 'iron' in its title to indicate that it had rails made of iron, as its freight was mostly agricultural produce, manure and coal. The horse-drawn freight services ceased in 1846 as other railways were constructed in the area.

Some railway stations were closed to regular passenger services very early on. Modifications to the Liverpool & Manchester Railway, that opened in 1830 and rapidly witnessed a massive growth in passenger traffic, resulted in Liverpool Crown Street closing to passengers in 1836, when trains were diverted to the larger Liverpool Lime Street. At the other end of the line Manchester Liverpool Road station, the oldest surviving closed station in Britain, closed to passengers in 1844 when it was replaced by the larger Manchester Victoria. Lancaster Greaves station, closed in 1849, also still survives, as does Curzon Street station in Birmingham, closed to regular passenger services in 1854 when New Street station was completed.

Manchester Liverpool Road station is the earliest purpose-built station to survive. It was opened in 1830 by the Liverpool & Manchester Railway and closed to passengers in May 1844, when services were extended into Manchester Victoria. The station remained in other rail uses until 1975 and has since become a museum. The frontage on Liverpool Road is viewed here in August 2016, shortly after rail access to the site had been cut. *Author*

The Liverpool & Manchester Railway's Crown Street terminus at Liverpool opened in 1830. It was the first station in the world to have a train shed, but also the first major station to close to passengers, in August 1836, when the larger Liverpool Lime Street station opened. The station buildings are no more, but the site remained in use for freight until May 1972. *Author's collection*

Edinburgh St Leonards station was reached by a tunnel opened in 1830, one of the first on a public railway in Scotland. Being located rather out of the city centre, the line closed to passengers in 1846 when more central routes developed. The southern portal of the 570yd (522m) tunnel is seen in September 2010. *Author*

In Edinburgh, in 1831, a line opened from St Leonards to coal mines in the Dalhousie area. Passengers were also conveyed and horse-drawn trains slowly ambling past Holyrood Park gave rise to the line being called the 'Innocent Railway'. Closure to passengers came in 1846 when more central stations were opened in Edinburgh.

In London, the development of the railway network saw early passenger closures as new, improved and expanded lines superseded old ones. The London & Southampton Railway's terminus at Nine Elms closed in 1848 when the line was extended to Waterloo. Bricklayers' Arms station closed in 1852 when most services were diverted to London Bridge and in 1875, the Bishopsgate terminus closed when services were extended into Liverpool Street.

There were also early closures underground in London. The Tower Hill Subway, which once had a 2ft 6in cable-hauled line, closed in 1894 when nearby Tower Bridge opened. In 1900, King William Street underground terminus closed when the current Northern Line was extended into north London.

Early closures were not limited to urban areas; the Newmarket & Chesterford Railway went bankrupt and closed in 1851. It was one the first significant passenger lines to close in Britain. Improvements to the route of the Dundee & Newtyle Railway saw some original sections of line close in 1855. The High Peak line in Derbyshire opened in 1832 and introduced a passenger service using the inclines, but this was neither profitable nor speedy. These passenger facilities ceased in this remote rural area in 1877, although freight continued for another 90 years.

Not all early lines resulted in early closures. In Scotland, a coal freight wagonway opened between Tranent and Cockenzie Harbour on the Firth of Forth in 1722. It is generally considered the first horse-operated wagonway in Scotland and was even used for cover in the Battle of Prestonpans during the Jacobite rising of 1745. The route, much of which had been converted into a railway, closed in 1959, although a section remained for wagon storage until 1963 when the last coal pit in this area closed.

Birmingham Curzon Street is the surviving northern terminus of the London & Birmingham Railway, which was the first long-distance main line opening in 1838. The imposing and decorated stone building, designed as an impressive classical gateway to the railway, was last used by regular passenger trains in 1854. The building is seen in August 2001. *Author*

Two early lines that are also now closed were particularly interesting. The Canterbury & Whitstable Railway opened in 1830. As well as having the first railway harbour, the first ever season tickets were issued in 1834. The Leicester & Swannington Railway opened in 1832, with the first train being driven by George Stephenson. Both railways were operated by steam from the outset and were the first two early lines to contain passenger tunnels. As with many lines that closed to passenger services in the 1920s and 1930s, they survived for freight for quite a while longer before complete closure.

Other early closures were due to competition from trams, with railway services to Govan at Glasgow closing in 1902, whilst passenger stations on the Paisley & Barrhead District Railway never even opened as Glasgow's trams were so popular. In 1911, the South Eastern Railway line through Rochester to Chatham Central was closed after this railway shared operations with the rival London, Chatham & Dover Railway to form the South Eastern & Chatham Railway.

Prior to World War 1 a relatively small number of lines had closed. However, during the war, by way of example over 2,500 employees of the GWR alone were killed, resulting in a shortage of railwaymen. The war also resulted in a scattering of local lines being closed across Britain. The Oldbury branch closed to passengers in 1915, together with the Addison Road–Hammersmith branch in 1916 and the South Acton–Hammersmith & Chiswick line in 1917. Furthermore, rails were requisitioned on some lines for the war effort. This resulted in the Portessie–Keith line being closed in 1915, together with the Basingstoke–Alton and Bideford–Appledore lines in 1917. Although all were closed as a temporary measure, when in 1918 the war ended, none of the lines reopened to passengers again. The exception was the Basingstoke–Alton line which reopened to passengers for a short period between 1924 and 1932.

*Right:* Two 70ft (21m) pointed neo-Tudor arches were cut into York's city walls to serve the original terminal station, opening within the city in 1841. The station was closed to passengers in 1877 when the present through station was constructed, although tracks remained for freight and storage until 1965. A hole in the wall to the old station is seen in September 2016. *Author*

*Opposite:* An era of horse-drawn wagonways preceded the railways and Cockenzie Harbour was served by a coal wagonway as far back as 1722, arguably the first in Scotland. The last sections of the railway, built on much of the wagonway's original route in the 1880s, were closed in 1963. However, some rails remained on the slip from a boatyard at Cockenzie Harbour in September 2010. *Author*

# 2
# Pre-Grouping stone

Once the railways became established, some generated good financial returns which encouraged new lines to be built. Many of the pre-Grouping companies were proud, self-confident and adventurous builders and this was reflected in numerous railway structures. There were periods of great prosperity and railways represented the biggest engineering project Britain had ever seen. Bridges and viaducts that could withstand the pounding of heavy locomotives and freight trains, without the need for speed restrictions, were required.

The use of stone for building has a long and deep-seated history. Consequently, particularly where locally available, it was used by the pre-Grouping railways for its strength, durability and low maintenance. The earliest railways used stone blocks as the 'sleeper' part of their track and the Haytor Tramway even used granite sections to guide wagons. Local stone was often removed from cuttings and utilised nearby to construct buildings and bridges.

The types of stone found locally varied considerably from hard granite to softer sandstone, all giving distinctive finishes. The CR used sandstone that exuded a soft reddish colour, such as at Edinburgh Princes Street, whilst in northern industrial areas some of the cream-coloured stone structures could turn black with weathering and soot. Golden yellow limestone, found at Mansfield, was used for the local station and for the Palace of Westminster. Aberdeen granite was a strong grey stone used at Aboyne station. Blue lias stone was used for Binton station near Stratford-on-Avon, whilst Lakeland green stone was used for Keswick station. Small knapped (split) flint stones were utilised to good effect for some stations in East Anglia, such as Swaffham.

Early cast iron rails were brittle and often broke under heavy weights. The Haytor Tramway on Dartmoor was a stone track tramway, opening in 1820 it brought granite down from a quarry at Haytor. Trucks were guided by grooves in the granite sets. Closed in 1858, part of the granite track was still clearly visible when this view was taken in September 1993. *Author*

Part of a former joint LYR & LNWR steam-operated hydraulic hoist that transported freight wagons to and from an adjoining freight yard at a higher level at Leeds Central station. Designed with both rough and smooth stone in the 1850s, the building fell out of use in the 1950s. It is seen in April 1996, looking rather like an ancient fort, and still remains. *Author*

Many railway bridges, viaducts and other railway buildings had a rustication finish, a rough surface, in a similar style to some of the great stone medieval castles. On the other hand, numerous stone station buildings were finely cut and smoothly faced. Considerable attention could go into the detailed design, ornamentation and appearance of such buildings. There was a huge range of individually designed stone railway buildings and whilst MR stone station buildings were increasingly built to a standard design, they were often individually constructed in various local stone.

Although the railways facilitated the transport of stone, it was utilised most in areas where it was found in abundance and stone viaducts represent one of the most spectacular achievements of the railways. The largest disused stone railway structures are some of the huge northern viaducts. The 17-arched mostly stone Hewenden Viaduct in Yorkshire, with its deep foundations, is a surviving treasure. Opening in 1883 the viaduct closed in November 1963 and is now part of the GNR trail for walkers and cyclists.

A mixture of stone was sometimes used to create visual effect. The attractive Victoria Viaduct over the River Wear was made from Penshaw sandstone, with Aberdeen granite dressings. The viaduct continued to be used by freight trains until 1991 and remains *in situ*. Stone, sometimes with brick top arches, was also used and in Wales, the nine-arched Cwm Prysor Viaduct, the 16-arched Hengoed Viaduct and the 15-arched curving Cefn Coed Viaduct are great remaining treasures.

In Scotland some parts of the landscape are sparse and bleak and viaducts can look particularly imposing and impressive. Those in the Borders include the 14-arched Teviot Viaduct at Roxburgh and Drygrange Viaduct, known also as Leaderfoot Viaduct. The latter, with its 19 arches, was built mainly in local red sandstone and is particularly striking. Although there are other wonderful contenders, Drygrange is one of my top 10 closed railway treasures.

The River Severn crossing opened in 1879 and showed that the most difficult of physical obstacles could be overcome by the railways. The remaining circular local limestone tower, that once housed the turning mechanism for the swing section over the Gloucester & Sharpness Canal, is seen in June 1993. The bridge closed after serious damage was caused by shipping using the River Severn in October 1960. *Author*

The massive Cefn Coed Viaduct on the ex-BM & LNWR Joint Railway near Merthyr Tydfil in July 2008. The 15 arches, built on a curve, rise up to 115ft (35m) above the Taf Fawr. The viaduct is the third largest in Wales and was opened in 1868. It was planned to be built entirely of local limestone, but a strike by stone masons resulted in bricks also being used. The last freight train working over the viaduct was in August 1966. *Author*

Lake Viaduct on the ex-LSWR main line, west of Okehampton, viewed in July 2016. When the line was widened to double-track, a second viaduct was built beside the original, to the same design and local granite. The dividing line between the two structures is still visible, the original 1874 viaduct being to the left of the view and the widened structure of 1878 seen on the right. *Author*

The Heads of Valleys line was built through difficult mountain terrain. The solid local stone construction is apparent from this September 2003 view of an underbridge which carried the line over a road to a now disused quarry near Clydach Gorge. The limestone-built stations at Clydach and Govilon also both survive. *Author*

Here at Liverpool local reddish sandstone was used for some bridges. Although a relatively soft stone to work, repairs were on occasions required and some are visible here in September 2006. This bridge is on the ex-CLC Liverpool docks line, which closed to remaining traffic in July 1975 and the trackbed is now used as the Liverpool Loop Line footpath. *Author*

Tavistock Viaduct was opened in 1889. It was built in grey granite and set on concrete foundations. The viaduct is up to 75ft (23m) high, has eight arches and is seen in September 1993. The line closed in May 1968 as part of the ex-LSWR Exeter–Plymouth main line. There are plans to reopen the Plymouth–Tavistock section and perhaps on to Okehampton. *Author*

Leaderfoot Viaduct in Scotland in June 2013. Opened in 1865, the 19 spans on elegant tapering piers were constructed from local red sandstone and rise up to a maximum of 126ft (38m) above the River Tweed. Passenger services ended in August 1948, whilst freight continued to use the viaduct until July 1965. *Copyright Alan Murray-Rust: Creative Commons Licence*

Some examples of smaller stone viaducts are also worthy of mention; Laigh Milton Viaduct opened in 1812 and closed in 1846. As such it is the oldest surviving closed railway viaduct, even though it was built on wood foundations. Kielder Viaduct was built to a skew design by Nicholson, a Newcastle mathematician. By means of geometrical technique, each block of masonry was individually shaped for its place in the structure.

There are also attractive stone bridges, forgotten relics of an enterprising age. The stone Guthrie Castle railway gate bridge, that conveyed the railway over an entrance to the Guthrie estate in Scotland, together with the Lady Wimborne Bridge in Dorset, are both particularly ornamented and are little treasures in their own right.

The limestone-faced bridge, known as the Lady Wimborne Bridge, is bridge No 66 on the Broadstone Junction–Ringwood line which opened in 1847. The bridge passed over the drive to Canford Manor and the ornate design was insisted upon by the owner. On his death, his son took over and with his wife became Lord and Lady Wimborne in 1880. The last train passed over the bridge in May 1977 and it is seen here in May 2017. *Author*

The clever use of stone is seen in October 2002 under this bridge at Port Dinorwic, now Y Felinheli, showing the skewed stone, a masterpiece of precise engineering. The Bangor–Caernarfon line was clearly well built by the LNWR in 1852. It closed to all traffic in January 1972, but consideration has been given on some occasions to possible reopening. *Author*

Melrose station is a refined Jacobean-styled building, designed by John Miller for the NBR. It has been described as the most handsome provincial station in Scotland. A bay window displays the versatility and quality of the stone building. The station, part of which is seen in March 1993, was closed in January 1969 and awaits reopening of the southern section of the Waverley route. *Author*

The sturdiness of stone has led to many structures surviving as demolition could be difficult and expensive. The greatest stone railway building that has been lost was the Euston Arch at the London terminus of the London & Birmingham Railway. It was a Doric stone masterpiece in a city where brick was mainly used for railway construction. Fortunately the stone station at the Birmingham terminus still survives, as do some demolished parts of the Euston Arch, and there are plans for its rebuilding – we can but wait.

London Euston entrance lodges showing some of the 72 destinations purported once to be reached from the terminal. The two stone lodges are almost all that remains of the original station and are seen in August 2001. The Euston Doric Arch at over 70ft (21m) in height was the greatest early stone monument to the railway age. It was demolished in 1963, in a shameful act of wanton destruction. *Author*

# 3
# Moving minerals

The main railway routes and coal-fields in 1904.

Britain had enormous mineral reserves and by 1904 the key heavy mining industries in terms of annual value were: coal £84 million, iron £13 million, stone £4 million, clay £1.7 million and slate £1.6 million. These figures need to be multiplied by over a hundred to give very approximate values for today. It was the mix of abundant minerals and the railway's ability to move heavy loads economically that facilitated the growth of the Industrial Revolution.

Coal was the traffic for which most of the earliest railways were built and the mass movement of coal developed around the relatively small, but well known, 10–12-ton four-wheeled wagon. It was used in multiples to create very heavy and long freight trains, sometimes requiring double-heading or banking assistance. Long rakes of unfitted wagons, even running at 25mph, tested many of the private coal wagons used. Some were in a poor state of repair until national maintenance standards were introduced.

In South Wales the rich coal reserves, including high quality anthracite, led to the densest mineral railway network ever created. Virtually every coal mine was connected to the railway network and production peaked in 1913, when the rail served Cardiff and Barry docks exported some 37 million tonnes of coal. Although South Wales became the largest coal exporting area in the world, coal exports from the Humber, Mersey and many other ports with rail links to coal pits, including those in Scotland, kept the railways both busy and mostly profitable. On the River Tyne, the Dunston Staithes were constructed to transfer coal to ships. The huge wooden railway pier is the largest in Europe and, as such, is one of my top 10 closed railway treasures.

The railways conveyed huge amounts of coal, which in the past was a mainstay of the profitability of many railways. Coal mines in South Wales were at one time a very common sight, together with the ubiquitous four-wheeled coal wagons. Today the only mines remaining are those preserved such as at Big Pit, the National Coal Museum of Wales, seen in February 2004. *Author's collection*

Cefn Coed Pit in South Wales is also now a museum. In September 2004 a 0-6-0ST Hunslet Austerity locomotive built by Bagnall and dating from 1944, was kept at the site. It was one of numerous small locomotives that were used to shunt trucks at coal mines and on the main line sidings. The pit, which once employed almost 1,000 men, ceased production in 1968. *Author*

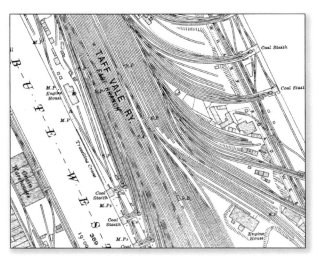

Coal sidings at Cardiff Bute Dock in 1920.
*Crown copyright reserved*

The site of Ynyshir station in the Rhondda Fach, in September 2003. Opened by the Taff Vale Railway in 1876, it was located on the once-busy Maerdy branch. The station closed in June 1964, but the line survived for coal traffic until August 1986. The track was taken up and the station demolished the following year. In 2005 the bridge was removed to make way for a new road. *Author*

A lost coal mine at Fernhill above Blaenrhondda in South Wales. Even when pictured here in August 1993, an old stationary boiler that had been used to generate steam for the mine could still be found. The tranquillity today belies the hive of activity that in the past went on here. *Author*

A gradual decline in output from the British coalfields was recorded for almost every year since the 1920s, as exports declined and oil became increasingly used. With this came a similar decline in the railways most dependent on coal. By the time of railway nationalisation in 1948, the Yorkshire, Midlands and Durham coalfields had all overtaken South Wales in coal production.

*Above left:* In keeping with their work, transport for miners was far from luxurious. These open-top knifeboard colliery worker's trucks ran directly into drift mines and are seen in County Durham at Beamish Museum in September 1999. The railways were a major and inseparable part of coal production, serving the pits on the surface and underground. *Author's collection*

*Above right:* The drift coal mine at Beamish Museum already existed on the site. Unlike pits, which required vertical lift shafts to reach the coal, drift mines ran into the coal seam from ground level on a generally parallel path to the mineral seam. The entrance is viewed from within the mine in September 1999. *Author's collection*

The coal drops at Shildon in October 2016. Coal wagons from local mines were hauled to the top of the stone wall and coal dropped into chutes which in turn filled locomotive tenders and other coal wagons below. The structure dating from 1856 is to be found on an original section of the Stockton & Darlington Railway. *Author*

THE SOUTH YORKSHIRE
JOINT LINE COMMITTEE
PUBLIC WARNING
ALL PERSONS ARE HEREBY WARNED NOT
TO TRESPASS ON THIS RAILWAY OR ON
ANY STATION OR OTHER WORKS LANDS
OR PROPERTY OF THE SOUTH YORKSHIRE
JOINT LINE COMMITTEE
ANY PERSON SO TRESPASSING IS LIABLE
TO A PENALTY OF FORTY SHILLINGS
BY ORDER

Millions of tonnes of coal would have passed under this unassuming bridge at Sykehouse in Yorkshire, seen in August 2008. It was one of over 40 bridges that were built on the Braithwell to Thorpe-in-Balne section of the ex-GC & HB Joint Railway that once conveyed coal from Yorkshire pits to Hull, in particular, for export. *Author*

Coal wagons at Prestongrange Industrial Heritage Museum, Scotland, in June 2011. The museum occupies the site of a colliery closed in 1962. Thousands of these wagons would have once been used. In some cases the wagons were also fitted with drop ends, or doors in the bottom, so that they could discharge directly into hoppers and coal drops. They were also equipped with individual hand brakes which could be pinned down by the guard. *Author's collection*

Attempts by the railways to introduce larger and faster wagons had mostly been thwarted by the coal owners. The small wagons were cheap to build, could operate over poor quality colliery lines, use existing wagon facilities and thus save on new investment. As a consequence, in 1948 BR inherited over half a million four-wheeled mineral wagons, the majority not even fitted with continuous brakes. For a while BR even built new wagons to similar designs, until it was realised that the future had to be with larger and faster wagons.

In 1958 there were about 1,500 coal mines; today coal is imported and there are no deep coal mines. The coal mines, large railway coal depots, such as those near Camden and King's Cross, small domestic railway coal merchant yards and the later coal concentration depots, all with their network of lines, have gone. Coal delivery to electricity generating stations by rail is expected to end by about 2023 and with this, the merry-go-round trains that have made the transport of coal by rail so efficient. It is likely that after over 200 years there is the prospect of very little coal being transported by rail.

The coalfields of Scotland became part of the Scottish NCB in 1947. The upper part of a colliery engine is seen at Prestongrange in June 2011. Railway-served coal mines survived in Scotland until the late 1990s. Coal was later imported, including via Leith Docks, but with coal-fired electricity power stations closing, the use of coal trains continues to diminish. *Author's collection*

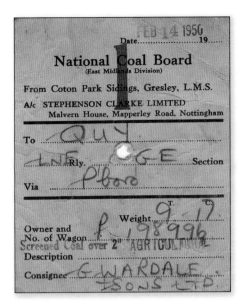

*Scaldwell*, 0-6-0ST Peckett locomotive, dating from 1913, is stored at Amberley Museum in June 1999. It was one of a number of 3ft narrow-gauge engines that transported iron ore from the Scaldwell opencast quarries in Northamptonshire to interchange sidings. The line closed in December 1962. The locomotive has since been donated to the Southwold Railway Trust. *Author*

Turning to iron ore, the Industrial Revolution created ever-greater demands for iron products. Iron ore was discovered in a number of areas and where it was found, particularly if in conjunction with nearby coal and limestone, the ingredients for making metals, it inevitably led to the development of iron and later steel works. Their growth became dependent on the railways from the narrow-gauge ironstone quarry lines, such as those at Kettering and Scaldwell, to a network of internal works lines, sometimes conveying molten metal.

When local ores were exhausted the expense of relocating iron and steel works was prohibitive. This worked in the railway's favour for a time by creating ever-longer journeys to supply iron ore, limestone and coal or coke, enabling some of the works to continue to operate for longer. For example, iron ore was conveyed from the Tyne to Consett until the works closed in 1980. Corby Steelworks closed at the same time, due in part to the low quality of the

Iron ore was found extensively in Britain. Florence No 2 Mine at Egremont in the Lake District was the last deep haematite mine in Western Europe, closing in 2007. Railway remains at the mine are seen in July 2009. It is a reminder that some parts of the Lakes at one time had heavy industries. *Author*

At Consett Steel Works in County Durham, molten steel was conveyed around the works by rail. This remaining hopper wagon lies in a park, as a reminder of Consett's industrial past, and is observed here in July 1966. Consett works closed in 1980, the last train ran in March 1984 and most traces of the works and its railways have since been removed. *Author*

remaining local iron ore. Iron ore deliveries to Dowlais ceased in 1987, whilst it was conveyed to Ravenscraig until this plant closed in 1992. The same was the case at Ebbw Vale; once the largest steel works in Europe, it survived on rail-delivered iron ore until its closure in 2002. Coastal locations reduced transport costs, but in 2015 Redcar Steelworks closed. Just as with coal mines, there seems an endless catalogue of iron and steel works closures which in turn produced a raft of associated railway closures, although the Ebbw Vale line reopened for passengers in 2008 and steel is still transported by rail.

China clay, also known as kaolin, was transported by rail from the mining areas to ports in Cornwall and at one time thousands of tonnes of this white clay were being extracted, particularly in the St Austell area. What became known as the Cornish Alps started to dominate the landscape, as for every tonne of usable clay produced, there were over five tonnes of waste. The china clay was for many years transported in

special tarpaulin-covered four-wheeled wagons. The GWR built some 500 of these wagons in 1913 and many remained in use until they were replaced in the early 1980s with larger wagons. The modern wagons still run to Carne Point, just short of Fowey Docks, but in reduced quantities.

Good quality building stone was found throughout Britain and railways were often used to convey stone, particularly to ports for onward transhipment by coastal shipping. For example at Portland, stone was conveyed on the steeply-inclined Merchant's Railway that opened in 1826 and remained in use until 1939. Of the many stone and sand quarries once served by railways, some still have rail access, including those used for track ballast, and heavy freight trains conveying stone, sand and aggregates can still be seen.

Although numerous mineral lines were built to standard-gauge, narrow-gauge lines were often found serving mines and quarries and were once widely used for

A China clay hood wagon at Torrington station in September 1995. A dedicated wagon fleet, that when loaded were covered with tarpaulins, once served this traffic and used this line until 1982, whilst formal closure came in March 1983. The Tarka Valley Railway have plans for reopening part of the line at Torrington. *Author*

At Leighton Buzzard, a 2ft narrow-gauge system developed to serve the local sand quarries. Opening in 1919, most commercial sand freight ceased in 1969, although a section remained until June 1981 and this is viewed here in January of that year. Today much of the original line is operated by the Leighton Buzzard narrow-gauge heritage passenger railway. *Author*

Welsh slate was found in difficult mountain terrain and produced many breath-taking railway inclines, such as the Vivian Quarry gravity-balanced transporter at Dinorwic. Loaded slate wagons hauled empty ones back up the gradient, as seen here in September 1999. Slate once roofed the world and for a time was known as 'grey gold'. *Author*

the extraction of mineral deposits. In the mountainous area of North Wales, massive slate quarries were established and those at Dinorwic and Penrhyn were the largest in the world. Elsewhere, such as at Nantle and Blaenau Ffestiniog, the landscape was also scarred by huge slate workings. The expansion of these slate workings was only made possible by the extensive use of flexible narrow-gauge railways; for example there were over 50 miles of line at the Dinorwic quarries. Narrow-gauge lines were also established to enable the slate to reach Welsh ports for export such as those at Dinorwic, Penrhyn, Caernarfon and Porthmadog.

The Ffestiniog Railway was at the forefront of narrow-gauge technology, allowing the slate trains to reach the coast simply by gravity and also developing articulated Fairlie locomotives with double boilers to provide a great deal of power within a confined loading gauge. By 1891, about 17,000 Welshmen were producing over half a million tonnes of slate a year, but after World War 2 the ever-growing competition from other roofing materials resulted in the closure of numerous quarries and all the remaining slate railways. Fortunately many narrow-gauge railways and some slate workings have since reopened as tourist attractions.

A 1ft 11½in-gauge slate GWR wagon seen at Llechwedd Slate Caverns in September 2003. A number of underground slate workings were to be found in North Wales. That at Aberllefenni ceased working in 2003 and marked the end of more than two centuries of narrow-gauge railways being used in the Welsh slate industry. *Author's collection*

*The Eclipse*, a 1ft 11½in-gauge electric locomotive at Llechwedd Slate Caverns in North Wales. Unusually it was originally a steam locomotive, but was rebuilt as an electric locomotive in 1927. It was in use until the 1960s and is seen at Llechwedd in September 2003. It has since been sent with a sister locomotive for restoration. *Author's collection*

# 4
# Railway bricks

Stone was not readily available in all parts of the country and the stonemason's skills became increasingly difficult to obtain. As a result, being cheaper to use than cut stone and a very versatile building component, bricks became the leading material used in railway construction.

At first local brickworks were used. This led to a rich variety of brick railway buildings, often fitting well into the area because of the use of locally coloured bricks. However, as demand increased, brickworks became larger, often being served by their own narrow-gauge network of lines, bringing clay to the kilns for firing and conveying the completed bricks to the main line siding for dispatch. The widespread transport of bricks by the railways reduced the distinctive local brick variations.

Stewartby station was in the heart of the Bedfordshire brick-making area and, when visited in May 1981, was oil lit. Unlike many large stations featured in this book it still remains, on a surviving section of the Oxford–Cambridge line, together with four of the many chimneys seen here, but brickmaking has ceased. *Author*

London Bishopsgate station closed to passengers in November 1875, when the line was extended to Liverpool Street. The Italianate-designed station became a goods depot until it was destroyed by fire in 1964. This part of the viaduct, pictured in September 1997, on which the station once stood, comprises a mixture of coloured brick and would have looked particularly striking when new. *Author*

London St Pancras Somers Town. The goods yard was built by the MR in a Gothic design to complement St Pancras station on the other side of the road. The bricks on the upper part of the wall were smaller to give a perception of greater height. The depot was closed in 1975 and the wall, seen in September 1997, has since been demolished. *Author*

The first mechanically produced bricks were made in 1855 and works soon became capable of producing 25,000 bricks a day with minimal labour. Railway companies even produced their own bricks such as the GWR at Swindon Works, the SER which set up a brick-making factory near Folkestone and the LNWR with its brickworks at Crewe and brickyards in Staffordshire.

The railways were largely hand built by an army of workmen. They embraced a range of abilities and the skilful usage of bricks can be found on many railway structures. Intricate patterns and the ornate use of different brick types and colours was common place. Haverthwaite and Stoke Golding are just two of many examples of stations built in a mixture of different coloured bricks. Diamond paver bricks were found routinely on platforms and on occasions terracotta bricks were used to make sculptured reliefs.

A Framlingham branch viaduct showing the layers of bricks that were to be found in many railway bridges and viaducts. This view was taken in July 1990. Although the adjoining embankment was taken down, the viaduct proved difficult to remove and still remains. It is now sometimes known locally as 'the bridge to nowhere'. *Author*

*Opposite:* Birmingham Snow Hill station. The brown glazed terracotta bricks were good for resisting staining by pollution and are viewed in August 2000. Some small parts of the GWR Snow Hill station still survive in an area mostly transformed by new development. In 1967 Snow Hill became an unstaffed halt and was closed in March 1972, only for a new station to reopen in 1987. *Author*

*Right:* The Bute Dock Company changed its name to the Cardiff Railway in 1897, when this building was completed. The view shows how very versatile terracotta bricks can be and how wealthy the company was at the time. The Welsh motto reads 'By Fire and Water'. This view, at Cardiff Pierhead, was taken in September 2003. *Author*

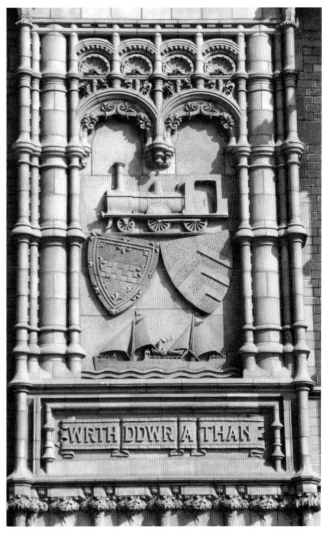

Although the principles of brick-built railway viaducts remained largely unchanged, many unique individual designs were constructed. The Braithwaite Viaduct in London completed in 1842, when viewed from underneath, provides a maze of interlocking arches, creating a form of pointed looking Gothic arches. A similar effect is to be found under Manchester Central station.

Red brick was widely used and in terms of large red brick-built structures on lost lines, a number of surviving viaducts are worthy of mention. The striking red brick viaduct at Larpool outside Whitby survives, is mentioned in Bram Stoker's *Dracula* novel and is a disused railway treasure. The red brick John O'Gaunt Viaduct on the GN&LNW Joint Railway has had its aesthetics disfigured by some spalled red bricks being replaced with blue engineering bricks. The same unsympathetic repairs were carried out on other viaducts, including that on the Alexandra Palace branch at Muswell Hill. Many station buildings were also built in red bricks; the GWR used red Ruabon bricks and it is one of the most widely used brick colours for railway buildings.

Some stations were distinctively made of very light, almost white bricks, such as Tattershall on the Lincolnshire Loop Line and Bartlow on the Cambridge–Colchester line. Whilst other stations on these lines were also made from light-coloured bricks, many were built in red or brown bricks as well. There are also a number of white brick viaducts and some two and a half million white fire bricks were used to build the graceful treasure of Hownsgill Viaduct near Consett. Underneath a number of railway bridges, in passenger subways and dimly lit areas, bricks with a white or cream glazed surface were sometimes used to enhance lighting.

The John O'Gaunt Viaduct on the ex-GN & LNW Joint Railway in Leicestershire closed to remaining traffic in June 1964 and is seen in August 2008. The 13 main arches are 60ft (18m) high and make an impressive sight in the landscape. Many of the spalled red bricks have been unsympathetically repaired with blue engineering bricks, as these were stronger. *Author*

The Big Water of Fleet Viaduct in Scotland had a huge amount of reddish brown bricks used to stabilise and encase the 19 stone piers of the original structure. Built on boggy land, movement was detected by the LMS and from 1927 much remedial work was undertaken. The viaduct, which was last used by a train in June 1965, is seen in July 2009. *Author*

Improvements in brick making methods continued with deep clays being used for dense engineering bricks. These bricks were of a consistent quality and of high compressive strength that absorbed little water. Blue Staffordshire brindle and other engineering bricks were used nationally from the 1870s to create very solid structures reflecting the ever-heavier loads operating on the railways. Good examples of blue engineering brick viaducts can be found on disused sections of the GCR. Several disused GWR lines in the Birmingham area are also mostly built from such bricks.

The viaduct at Greenock leading to James Watt Dock on the Clyde shows that even the most mundane of dock viaducts were sometimes decorated. Cream glazed bricks were interspersed with brown by the CR and are observed here in September 2010, just prior to demolition. James Watt was born in Greenock. *Author*

A station chimney stack showing the decorated brickwork at Mayfield in Sussex in April 1995. The attractive brick detailing was provided by the LBSCR at some stations, whilst a number of their rural stations were built to an appealing country house-style. *Author*

Part of the glazed wall used to display a map of the LYR network, at Manchester Victoria station in September 1991. The map dates from 1904 and shows many lost lines, but has been sensibly retained. Tile maps of the LBSCR have been retained at London Victoria and a number of tile maps of the NER also remain, including one at York station. *Author*

White-faced structural glazed bricks were provided in a passage that connected the High Level and now closed Low Level stations at Wolverhampton, in August 2000. The white surface reflected light and thus they were used under bridges and in dimly lit passageways in particular. *Author*

Cannington Viaduct on the Lyme Regis branch in Dorset was 92ft (28m) high and is seen here in September 1995. The LSWR-built concrete viaduct suffered subsidence and this delayed its opening until 1903. An arched infilling of yellow bricks prevented any further movement. The viaduct has not been used for trains since November 1965. *Author*

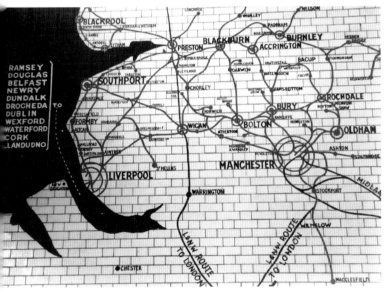

*Above:* South Bermondsey station was until 1869 called Rotherhithe. The station closed in June 1928 when a new station was opened. The distinctive LBSCR red, yellow and black coloured bricks were still apparent when this view was taken in May 1998. This brickwork must have looked lovely when new. *Author*

*Left:* A section of the approach viaduct to Bishopsgate with side-arch supports in September 1997. The London yellow stock brick viaduct was perhaps not an ideal colour for use next to a busy steam railway out of Liverpool Street in London. The viaduct, which was last used in December 1964, still survives. *Author*

Although bricks became the preferred method of railway construction and supplanted stone, they were often used in conjunction with other building materials including stone, iron and wood. Iron components were sometimes added to provide strength to large brick buildings such as railway warehouses.

The tall chimneys associated with the brick kilns became a common part of the landscape. However, once the clay was exhausted, they mostly became disused and water-filled clay pits, derelict buildings, rusting tramways and overgrown railway sidings could once be found in almost every county.

The Grand Union Canal passes under the substantial blue brick Duddeston Viaduct in Birmingham, seen in August 2001. The viaduct was built by the GWR to connect with other railways to the north at Curzon Street, but the newly formed LNWR prevented this access and the viaduct was never used for anything more than a head shunt. *Author*

Blackpool Central was partly built on an elevated site and some of the retaining walls, built in blue engineering bricks, were strengthened by a blind arch as seen here in July 2009. On August Bank Holiday in 1910, almost 100 mostly mill workers excursion trains used the station and it was still busy when it closed in November 1964. *Author*

As a postscript, the waterproofing of brick structures is important, as the seepage of water, particularly when combined with frost, can damage brick structures. In my view, although not compromising safety, not enough routine maintenance is being carried out by Network Rail and small trees and bushes can be seen growing out of many brick structures on lines that are in use. A backlog of regular maintenance is likely to result in massive repair bills in the future.

The ex-CLC Liverpool dock route near West Derby in September 2006. The skewed brick bridge arch, almost looking unfinished, demonstrates the versatility of brick structures. The bridge was also designed so any quadrupling of the line could be accommodated with minimal disruption. As it turned out, this was not required; the line was last used in July 1975, and is now a footpath. *Author*

The smaller viaduct on the GWR Camerton branch passed under the substantial, 50ft (15m) high, blue engineering brick Midford Viaduct, which was built by the S&D when this section was widened to double-track in 1903. The branch was the location for the *Titfield Thunderbolt* film and track remained until 1958, whilst the larger viaduct remained in use until March 1966. The structures are pictured in March 2009. *Author*

Bricks were extensively used for tunnel construction. The brick arch dates back to ancient times and is hugely strong. The Welsh arched tunnel entrance, seen in September 2003, has up to 10 rings of blue bricks. This immensely strong construction was designed to try and prevent any distortion that could be caused by mining subsidence in the area. *Author*

# 5
# Metal masterpieces

When railway lines closed, station buildings and land could be relatively easily sold off, but solid viaducts and bridges were another matter. Metal viaducts and bridges have fared least well, as after closure they were seen as a continued burden to maintain for safety reasons and a valuable source of scrap.

Before steel became available, some accidents were caused by the brittleness of early cast iron bridges failing under the increasing weight of trains and limited numbers survive today. The earliest surviving metal railway bridge is the cast iron Gaunless Bridge built for the Stockton & Darlington Railway in 1823, now preserved at the NRM at York.

Metal lattice girder bridges were increasingly used particularly from the 1860s; they were often built of riveted wrought iron, which was better in tension and ranged from larger structures to small span footbridges. The collapse of Bouch's Tay Bridge, in part due to some poor-quality cast iron, sent shock waves through the railways and several of his other bridges were strengthened as a precautionary measure. Equally, after the disaster rigid testing of bridges was undertaken. The Garmouth Viaduct in Scotland over the River Spey, with its 350ft central span, was loaded with 400 tonnes of gravel in 20 wagons before opening.

Many metal bridges were built on retaining walls of brick or stone. They were mainly functional, but

Loch Ken Viaduct in Scotland consists of three wrought iron bowstring girder spans, each 138ft (42m) long, over Loch Ken. It was constructed by the Portpatrick & Wigtownshire Joint Railway in 1861. The viaduct escaped demolition following the Stranraer–Dumfries 'Port Road' closure in June 1965 and is seen in July 2009. *Author's collection*

The Duke of Beaufort Bridge over the River Wye once carried the GWR Monmouth Troy–Monmouth May Hill line. The main 150ft (46m) lattice span, which dates from 1874, was last used by freight trains in October 1964 and is pictured in September 2003. Even without paint the bridge may take some time to rust through and is now used as a footpath and cycleway. *Author*

The 278ft (85m) long wrought iron lattice girder bridge over the River Spey at Ballindalloch in Scotland. The GNSR bridge plate records that it was built in 1863 by G. McFarlane of Dundee. Whisky trains once used this bridge before closure in November 1968. The bridge is now part of the long-distance Speyside Way and is seen in October 2011. *Author*

occasionally decoration was used such as that at Murrayfield on the ex-CR Edinburgh–Leith line. Metal bridges need painting to avoid corrosion, but some of the Victorian structures were so sturdy that even in a rusty state they remain structurally sound.

In 1858 Bessemer produced steel which was much stronger than iron, eventually creating new opportunities for railway engineers. Once steel was widely used, engineering structures became generally tougher, safer and often more impressive and by the 20th century steel had mostly replaced wrought iron for railway bridges.

A large steel lattice bridge, one of two, on the ex-CLC route to the docks at Liverpool and to Aintree, that were erected in the 1930s to cross major new roads that were being built at the time. The bridge spans the A580 and was last used by trains in July 1975. It is now used by the footpath and cycleway known as the Liverpool Loop Line, and is seen in September 2006. *Author*

Meldon Viaduct used cast iron, wrought iron and steel. The legs in turn support an upper Warren truss, seen here in July 2016. At its highest point the viaduct is 151ft (46m) above the river. Although the viaduct had been strengthened on four occasions since its opening by the LSWR in 1874, speed and weight restrictions were applied before tracks were finally removed in 1990. *Author*

Of metal viaducts that have been dismantled, the longest was the 193-span, over-1-mile-long, wrought and cast iron Solway Viaduct. The viaduct opened in 1869, closed in August 1921 and was demolished by 1935. The wrought and cast iron Crumlin Viaduct in South Wales, at 200ft (61m) in height, was the tallest in Britain. The line over the viaduct closed in June 1964 and although the structure was recognised as being of historic importance, it was demolished by 1967. Belah Viaduct in the Pennines was almost as high at 196ft (60m). It was also a fantastic example of a wrought and cast iron viaduct, but was dismantled for scrap together with other metal structures on the route after the line closed. Metal viaducts were mostly lighter than those built of stone or brick and could be less prone to ground subsidence. The wrought and cast iron Bennerley Viaduct near Derby and Meldon Viaduct near Okehampton in Devon are the last two metal trestle survivors and, as such, are both included

as being in my top 10 closed railway treasures.

There were several types of movable metal railway bridges that allowed clearance over navigable waters. A retractable disused railway bridge remains over the River Parrett at Bridgewater and a former road and rail bascule bridge at Birkenhead, but swing bridges were most widely used by the railways. Lost swing bridges include those provided as part of much larger structures. Examples embrace that provided on the Severn Railway Bridge over the Gloucester & Sharpness Canal. The slender complete 4,163ft (1,269m)-long wrought iron bridge opened in 1879, but was damaged by shipping in October 1960 and was demolished, together with the swing section, by 1970. The 1,610ft (490m) viaduct and swing bridge over the River Forth near Alloa opened in 1887. The bridge was closed in May 1968 and the metal decking and swing section removed, but most of the metal braced stone legs still survive.

Sharpness Dock High Level Swing Bridge provides a reminder of the general shape of the former River Severn railway bridge spans, being built by the same railway and opening in 1879. The wrought iron span at the north end of the dock is seen in June 1993. Freight trains no longer use the bridge, but a road does. The Vale of Berkeley Railway have long term aims to take over the Sharpness branch. *Author*

Fortunately a number of distinctive former railway swing bridges remain long after rail use ceased, including that over the navigable River Nene at Sutton Bridge, also known as Cross Keys Bridge. Signal leavers and equipment for this swing bridge were provided in 1897 and remain in use, although no longer connected to the signal boxes each side of the now all-road bridge. The railway swing bridge at Sharpness Dock has also been converted to road use.

Sculcoates Swing Bridge over the River Hull survives and is operational, although the trackbed has been converted to a footpath. Non-functioning former railway swing bridges are also to be found and range from the huge Victoria Swing Bridge at Leith to the small swing bridge over the Sheepwash Channel at Oxford. The latter was originally designed by George Stephenson and last used in 1984, but retains its swing mechanism and is to be restored to use.

Tower Road Bridge is a bascule lifting bridge at Birkenhead Docks. The bridge was originally powered from a central hydraulic engine house operating a counter balance. Dating from the 1930s, there was a 4mph speed restriction for trains crossing the steel bridge. The bridge is viewed in April 2006, but was demolished in 2017. *Author*

The swing Cross Keys, or Sutton Bridge, over the navigable River Nene was opened by the M&GN in 1897. The steel girder bridge has, since February 1959, been used entirely by road transport and remains operational, using much original equipment. Part of the turning mechanism is viewed from the wooden control tower in August 1994. *Author*

Other former railway bridges have been converted to road use such as Connel Ferry Bridge in Scotland, which was built in steel and opened in 1903. At the time, the bridge had the longest span of any railway bridge, excluding the Forth Bridge. The dramatic location, over the swirling sea entrance to Loch Etive, makes this bridge one of my top 10 closed railway treasures. The heavy steel truss Queen Alexandra Bridge at Sunderland opened in 1909 and had both road and rail decks. For a short period before World War 1, trains transported six million tonnes of coal a year over the bridge, but rail traffic ceased in 1921.

The swing bridge between Sculcoates and Wilmington at Hull remains operational, but in use as a footpath. The steel bridge, with a wooden control cabin located over the tracks, was opened in 1907 by the NER and replaced an earlier single-line structure. The Victoria Dock branch closed to remaining traffic in March 1969 and the bridge is seen in July 1996. *Author*

The former swing bridge at Naburn, south of York, opened in 1871 and one of the two wrought iron plate spans is seen in July 1996. In October 1983, a new ECML diversionary route was brought into use and the swing bridge became disused. The control cabin has been removed, whilst the bridge is now used by a footpath and cycleway. *Author*

Connel Ferry Bridge, viewed in July 2013, is a 524ft (160m) steel cantilevered bridge over the Falls of Lora, where the flood tide creates the effect of a waterfall. Originally the bridge carried the Ballachulish branch which was opened by the CR in 1903. A toll road was squeezed beside the railway in 1914, but since closure of the line in March 1966 the bridge has been exclusively used by road traffic. *J. Gray*

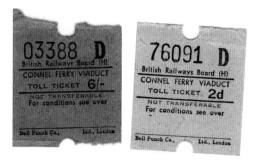

Blackfriars Bridge across the Thames was provided with huge decorative cast iron crests of the London, Chatham & Dover Railway and one is seen in September 1997. A similar ornate crest is preserved at Fawley Hill near Henley. The transfer of main line services into Waterloo resulted in a decline in the use of the first bridge, whilst a later bridge remains. *Author*

The Southport & Cheshire Lines Extension Railway opened in 1884 and this bridge at Mossbridge survived the station which closed in January 1917. The sturdy metal legs of the bridge are seen from the former railway trackbed in September 2006. The Trans Pennine Trail, a long-distance cycleway and footpath, now uses the trackbed here. *Author*

Blackfriars Bridge cast iron legs were filled with concrete and built on the foundations of the old Westminster road bridge. The original railway bridge over the Thames here opened in 1864 and was in use until February 1964, although decking remained until 1984. The third legs to the right of the view have been incorporated in an expanded Blackfriars station since this view was taken in September 1997. *Author*

Derby Friargate Bridge dates from 1878 and the ribbed cast iron arches were bolted together. The ornamental nature of the GNR-built bridge reflected the fact that it crossed one of Derby's most wealthy roads. The line closed in May 1968 and the bridge was taken over by the council. It is seen in September 2016. *Author*

The destructive decades of the 1960s and 1970s are for the most part over. The attractive designs and quality of build of many remaining metal railway structures are such that Historic England and the Welsh and Scottish equivalents have protected a number of important surviving metal viaducts and bridges. Elsewhere, local councils and other organisations have stepped in with the aim of retaining and making disused metal viaducts and bridges accessible to the public as walkways, or as part of a network of cycleways.

Part of a lengthy wrought iron lattice footbridge over the ex-GNR, M&GN and GN & GE Joint Committee alignments at St John's Road, south of Spalding station, in July 2008. The c1860 arches above the footway may once have supported lamps and also would have added strength. *Author*

On the Norwich–Melton Constable line an unusual 'A'-framed riveted steel girder bridge, No 249 and dating from 1882, was provided over the River Wensum at Hellesdon. This is now on a well-used section of the Marriott's Way footpath and is seen in October 2012. The 'A' frame gave additional strength to the bridge and it is one of two surviving such ex-M&GN bridges. *Author*

South of Honing station in Norfolk is this elegant bridge, built in steel and wrought iron as there was a shortage of bricks at the time. Dating from 1881 and later partly reconstructed, it is seen in November 2012. The structure is decorated with trefoil patterns and now bridges the Weavers' Way, a long-distance footpath that uses the trackbed of the ex-M&GN route here. *Author*

# 6
# Underground undertakings

Dudley Tunnel was opened in 1850 and construction was overseen by I. K. Brunel. It was last used for freight in March 1993. The interior of the 948yd (866m) tunnel is seen in August 2001. At this time mothballed track was still *in situ*, but steel gates have since been installed to prevent unauthorised entry to the tunnel. *Author's collection*

Although buried underground, tunnels represent some of the most enterprising and heroic works of railway civil engineering. There is some contention over the first railway tunnel in Britain. The Fritchley Tunnel on the Butterley Gangroad, a horse-drawn wagonway bringing limestone to an iron works near Crich and dating from 1793, is often considered one of the first. Indeed, several of the early railway tunnels were originally used by canals or wagonways and then converted to railway use.

Of the hundreds of railway tunnels constructed underground in Victorian times, many entrances are now lost under landfill, or sealed for safety reasons. The heavy and often dangerous work of tunnelling was done by men who were known as navvies. There were collapses and deaths, but gradually construction methods improved. It is estimated that there are about 600 lost railway tunnels in Britain, excluding those in mines.

Newcastle Quayside, with the entrance to the curving NER-built tunnels that totalled some 662yd (605m) up to Manors station, when this view was taken in July 1996. Opened in 1870, a section was built over the Victoria Tunnel, a lengthy 1842 wagonway tunnel. Between 1906 and 1964, electric freight trains used the 1 in 30 steeply-graded tunnels. Diesel traction then took over until closure in June 1969. *Author*

Privett Tunnel in Hampshire on the Meon Valley Alton–Fareham line, with a view taken in February 1985. The 1,058yd (967m) tunnel was opened in 1903 by the LSWR and was built to main line standards. The tunnel closed in February 1955 and the last remaining parts of the line closed in 1968. It is sometimes said that Privett Tunnel has its own ghost. *Author*

The twin 69yd (63m) Slade Tunnels on the Barnstaple–Ilfracombe line. The original single-line tunnel was opened by the LSWR in 1874 and a second added in 1891 as traffic grew. The line closed in October 1970, although track through the tunnel was not removed until 1975. One of the disused tunnels is now used as a footpath. The view was taken in September 1995. *Author*

A number of disused early treasures are to be found. Those built by the Liverpool & Manchester Railway in 1830 at Liverpool still survive under the city. The Tyler Hill Tunnel on the Canterbury & Whitstable Railway also opened in 1830. The Glenfield Tunnel, built for the Leicester & Swannington Railway, was the first over a mile in length used by passengers, opening in 1832. Some of the Liverpool & Manchester Railway tunnels were double-track, but most early tunnels were single-line with a restricted span, which caused problems as the size of locomotives and stock increased.

Within a few years of the earliest tunnels being built, the first tunnel was constructed under the Pennines at Woodhead in 1845 and at that time was the longest in Britain. A second adjoining single-line tunnel was built in 1853. The constant bombardment by steam and soot from locomotives in the confined single bores resulted in a deterioration of the tunnel's linings. As a consequence, a new double-track Woodhead Tunnel suitable for electrification was built between 1949–53 and was the most outstanding civil engineering achievement of BR, costing some £4.25 million. Sadly this hidden treasure was to face closure in July 1981. As a result, some of the longest closed main line tunnels in Britain are the old and new tunnels at Woodhead, all being in excess of three miles in length.

Lost tunnels over a mile in length in England also include the GCR Bolsover Tunnel; built in 1905 mainly for coal traffic, it closed in December 1951. The tunnel had suffered some movement and subsidence as a result of

Wapping Tunnel at Liverpool on the Liverpool & Manchester Railway. The plain western portal entrance reflects earlier canal practice and is seen in October 2006. The 1-mile 460yd (2,030m) length and 17ft (5m) span was the first railway tunnel of this scale, opening in 1830. It provided freight access to Liverpool Docks. The tunnel fell out of regular use in 1965 and was officially closed in May 1972. *Author*

Glenfield Tunnel in Leicestershire opened in July 1832. The 1-mile 36yd (1,642m) tunnel had a restricted span of 11ft 6in (3m) which prevented some later stock using the line. Engineered by the Stephensons, it was at the time the longest tunnel in the world used by a steam passenger railway. Additional ventilation shafts were added after opening. The tunnel closed in April 1966 and the western portal is pictured in September 1993. *Author*

*Right:* A ventilation chimney on the Wapping Tunnel at Liverpool in September 2006. The chimney vents cleared smoke after the tunnel was converted from rope to steam haulage. Such vents became a feature of most tunnels and were usually located over the vertical shafts sunk as part of the tunnel construction. The tunnel is disused, but remains intact. *Author*

*Below:* Trackbed leading to the eastern portal of the 3-mile 66yd (4,888m) Woodhead Tunnel at Dunford Bridge in September 1994. In 1954 the new tunnel was opened on the equally newly electrified line. The modern tunnel, the greatest engineering achievement of BR, was not to survive and closed in July 1981. *Author*

Queensbury Tunnel in Yorkshire was on the line serving Bradford, Halifax and Keighley. Opened in 1879, the 1-mile 741yd (2,287m) tunnel was at the time the longest on the GNR. It was last used in May 1956. The rubble seen in May 2007 has been tipped down the ventilation shaft when it was capped. There have been proposals to use the tunnel as a cycle route. *Copyright phill.d: Creative Commons Licence*

A ventilation shaft penetrates the brick arch, which is supported on stone sidewalls inside Queensbury Tunnel in May 2007. Five ventilation shafts were used, the deepest of which is 126yd (115m) and the largest in diameter is 4yd (3.6m). The shafts cut through coal, shale and sandstone; as a consequence water flowing down the shafts could form icicles in winter. *Copyright phill.d: Creative Commons Licence*

local mining and after an abortive effort to backfill the tunnel the entrances were sealed. Queensbury Tunnel was opened in 1878 by the GNR. It closed to passenger traffic in May 1955 and to freight a year later. Drewton Tunnel on the HB, which took four years to build, being completed in 1885, closed in December 1958. Catesby, Gildersome and Wenvoe tunnels were also all over a mile in length and were closed in the 1960s.

The wealth of coal and topography of the valleys in South Wales have led to a number of lengthy closed tunnels. Rhondda Tunnel, north of Treherbert, which took five years to construct, opened in 1890. It is the longest at almost two miles (3,148m) and also the deepest closed

Welsh tunnel, at almost 1,000ft (350m) below ground, services ceasing in February 1968. The Merthyr or Abernant Tunnel, between Merthyr and Abernant, dating from 1853 and designed by I. K. Brunel, was 650ft (198m) below ground at its deepest point. It is hoped both might one day be reopened for cycle routes. Elsewhere in Wales, the Torpantau Tunnel is at the highest altitude of any in Britain.

In Scotland the railways were mainly constructed to travel through valley passes and climb over higher ground, resulting in surprisingly few tunnels. Whitrope, on the Waverley route, is the longest closed tunnel. However, there are disused urban tunnels under both Glasgow and Edinburgh.

*Opposite:* The 674yd (616m) Talyllyn Tunnel in Wales, although expanded in size in 1863, dates from 1816 and was originally built for the Hay Railway, a horse-drawn route. As such, it was the oldest non-mining tunnel to survive in use until May 1964. At 1,313ft (400m) above sea level it was also the highest tunnel in Britain. The eastern stone portal is viewed in September 2003. *Author*

The 1-mile 736yd (2,283m) Merthyr Tunnel in South Wales suffered from mining subsidence. As a consequence the western portal roof has been reinforced with engineering bricks, as observed in September 2003. Opened in 1853, it is the second longest closed tunnel in Wales and ran on a descending gradient to Merthyr Tydfil. Also known as the Abernant Tunnel, it closed in December 1962. *Author*

The short tunnel at the Aberglaslyn Pass in North Wales, viewed here in September 1987. The 10yd (9m) tunnel was built in 1922 to a loading gauge that would allow for electrification of the line. There are few unlined passenger tunnels in Britain and this one is now back in use on the narrow-gauge Welsh Highland Railway. *Author*

Although some large coal mines had miles of subterranean lines, in London the 2ft-gauge Post Office Railway ran some 6½ miles underground from Paddington to Whitechapel, via Mount Pleasant. Opening in 1927 to transport mail in central London between sorting offices and main line stations, it closed in May 2003. It is the longest closed tunnel in Britain, but a section reopened as a tourist attraction in 2017.

An original Channel Tunnel was started in 1881 under the auspices of Sir Edward Watkin, who had plans to link the tunnel with the line to Sheffield and Manchester. The tunnel ran for well over 6,000ft (1,830m) under the sea from Shakespeare Cliff and was designed to meet a French counterpart tunnel being built out under the Channel from Sangatte. However, the government became worried about the military implications and the project was brought to a halt in 1883.

In more recent years, a number of disused tunnels have reopened as footpaths and cycleways; examples include that at St Leonards in Edinburgh, those in the Peak District and on the S&D at Combe Down. Occasionally tunnels such as that at Caernarfon and at Pinnock, the longest tunnel in Cornwall, are used as roads. Even a tunnel on the narrow-gauge Leek & Manifold Railway is used as a local road. Finally, the Connaught Tunnel in London Docklands has been brought back into railway use as part of the Crossrail project, whilst the tunnels at Aberglaslyn are again used by the heritage Welsh Highland Railway.

Whitrope Tunnel is 1,208yd (1,105m) long, opening in 1862 and one of only a few tunnels to be found in Scotland. The presence of a stream above the tunnel mouth led to instability and substantial retaining walls were provided on each side of the approach cutting. Located on the Waverley route which closed in January 1969, the tunnel is seen in March 1993. *Author*

The subterranean platforms at Botanic Gardens station, on the Central Glasgow Railway, were located between the 220yd (201m) Botanic and 711yd (650m) Great Western Road tunnels. Both daylight and ventilation were provided by the white glazed brick shaft. Opened in 1896, the station closed in February 1939, although trains used the line until October 1964. The surface of the station is seen in October 2011. *Author*

The 143yd (130m) Alloway Tunnel viewed from the River Doon Viaduct entrance in October 2011. The GSWR-built tunnel was to conceal the railway from the famous nearby Alloway Auld Kirk in Ayrshire. Opened in 1906, it closed in September 1968 and now provides a wide pedestrian tunnel. *Author*

Crystal Palace High Level with the ornate southern portal to the 439yd (401m) tunnel. This portal was particularly impressive because it faced the SECR terminal station. Built in 1865, the tunnel was called the Paxton Tunnel in tribute to the creator of the nearby Crystal Palace. The last train used the tunnel in September 1954 and the portal is pictured in May 1995. *Author*

The short Aldwych–Holborn tube line opened in 1907. It closed in September 1994, as a branch of the Piccadilly Line, when this view was taken on the last day of services at Aldwych. Although many underground stations are closed on lines that remain open, it was very rare to find the closure of an entire underground line in a busy city at this time. *Author*

The last train prepares to leave Aldwych for Holborn on 30 September 1994, almost 87 years after the opening of the line. The station was originally called Strand and this name could still be found inscribed in the tiles on closure. Lack of investment in that new lifts were required was given as the main reason for closure of this central London route. *Author*

A worker's refuge in the concrete interior of the 164yd (150m) Swainsley Tunnel, on the narrow-gauge Leek & Manifold Valley Light Railway, noted in June 1999. The tunnel was built to conceal the railway from Swainsley Hall. Opened in 1904, the line was closed by the LMS in March 1934. During World War 2 munitions were stored in the tunnel and the entrances sealed, but today it is used by a local road. *Author*

The single-line Combe Down Tunnel was opened in 1874 on the S&D. At 1-mile 69yd (1,672m) it became the longest unventilated tunnel on the BR network, which on occasions caused problems for steam locomotive footplate crew. The tunnel closed in March 1966 and is seen in March 2009. It has since reopened as a walkway and is currently the longest tunnel used by cyclists. *Author*

The 168yd (154m) Brinnington Number 2 Tunnel east of Brinnington Junction on the line that once ran through Stockport Tiviot Dale. The tunnel, on a rising curve, was opened in 1863 and was officially abandoned in 1982. It is seen in July 2009 and, as with an increasing number of disused railway tunnels, is now used by cyclists and pedestrians. *Author*

The 163yd (149m) Caernarfon Tunnel, on the Bangor–Afon Wen route, was provided in 1871 by the LNWR under the historic Y Maes (Castle Square) in the centre of the town. The line was last used in July 1969 for the storage of trains during the Investiture of the Prince of Wales. In 1999 the railway tunnel was converted into use as a road and is seen here in October 2002. *Author*

# Goods service withdrawn

The railways developed for freight because they proved to be cheaper and more reliable than the roads and quicker than the canals. One of the first significant purpose-built general railway goods yard was at Park Lane in the south of Liverpool Docks, opening in 1830. By 1900 Britain had over 22,000 miles of railway, all served by a multiplicity of goods yards, a myriad of sidings and industrial lines. Horses were regularly used for shunting wagons and cranes used for heavy lifting, but cheap manual labour was extensively used to load and unload wagons.

At their zenith, almost everything that could be moved was moved by rail and the railways operated a very diverse collection of goods facilities. At one time all kinds of goods from fragile eggs to huge 275-tonne boilers were

Cadbury once conveyed its products by rail and a chocolate biscuit factory at Moreton on the Wirral had its own shunting engine. The Hudswell Clarke locomotive, No 14 dating from 1956, is viewed outside the factory. The railway was out of action when this view was taken in October 2006. The diesel locomotive was eventually moved to Cadbury World at Bournville, whilst this factory closed in 2011. *Author*

*Below:* The MR-built grain warehouse No 2 at Burton-on-Trent dates from the 1880s. The building shows the once close link between the railways and the brewing industry. The area around the building previously embraced a coal yard, sidings and malt houses. This view was taken in September 1993 and today the warehouse is used as a hotel. *Author*

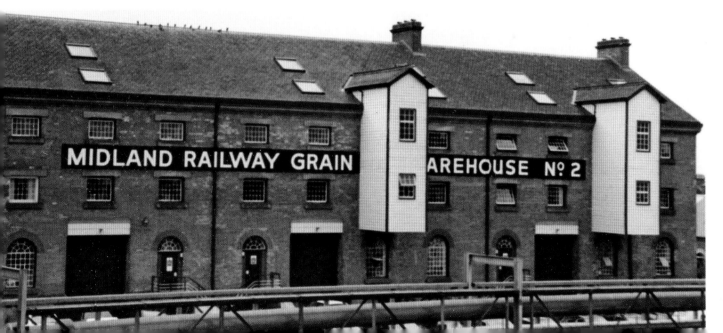

transported by rail. Circuses travelled round by rail; house and complete farm moves were all undertaken by the railways. Train ferries allowed goods wagons to be conveyed on ships and some goods travelled long distances.

The industrial siding developed as a widespread feature of the railways, ranging from a single siding to a private network of lines. There were many examples, such as the Bass Brewery at Burton-on-Trent, with about 16 miles of line, to the gas works at Beckton with almost 70 miles of line. Elsewhere, many larger firms used their own locomotives and wagons. Each of the thousands of stations on the railway network were also mostly equipped with goods sidings and frequently with a goods shed, loading crane, cattle dock and other facilities.

There was also a huge pool of rolling stock to transport the different types of goods. For example, there were vast numbers of open wagons, flat wagons and covered vans. These were added to by rolling stock for milk and other liquids, horses and other livestock, fish and seasonal agricultural goods, together with stock to provide for a wide range of other specialised goods from salt to bananas. Wagons for parcels and those for extra-large loads were all provided. In addition, there was an extensive variety of departmental rolling stock.

*Below:* The Cardiff dock warehouse of the LNWR at Tyndall Street once had five tracks leading into it. After closure and a period of dilapidation, it is now used as a hotel. The view, in September 2003, of the interior of the building, shows that it retains huge iron columns. They are a reminder of the strength required in a building once used to store heavy goods. *Author*

*Above:* Birmingham cattle station at Bordesley served the bull and cattle markets. The section of viaduct seen here, in August 2001, over Adderley Street was not used as the main line intended. At one time about 1½ million live cattle were transported by rail each year in Britain. Although this freight ceased here in 1964, the faded GWR 'ghost' sign was still visible. *Author*

*Below:* The GWR-built red brick goods shed at Tettenhall, near Birmingham, still survives. These were some of the last traditional-styled GWR buildings to be constructed in the 1920s, but closed in October 1932. The GWR painted initials have been removed from the side of the building, as seen in August 2001. *Author*

**(P. 1168) THE HIGHLAND RAILWAY.**

## LIVE STOCK.

Loaded. Date_____ Time_____

### From INVERNESS
## To SYMINGTON, CAL.
### Via DUNKELD, CAL

Consignee_____ Truck_____
Watered and (or) fed at_____ Time_____ Date_____
   „   „   „   at_____ Time_____ Date_____
                                    PAID         TO PAY
Carriage Charges ·  ·  ·  .  ·  ·  ·

A box van at Snape on the Suffolk coast seen in August 1994. Redundant goods vehicles such as this were sometimes used for agricultural and storage purposes. The Snape branch was always freight only and mainly provided barley to Snape Maltings. Opened in 1859 and closed in March 1960, the station building and maltings remain. *Author*

The railways were extensively used during World War 1. In addition to troops and horses, thousands of tonnes of munitions and supplies were sent particularly to the south coast ports for shipment to the front line in France. During World War 1 the better utilisation of railway goods wagons was also achieved by the collaboration of railway companies under government control. The lessons learnt led to the Grouping of 1923 and created the Big Four railway companies. This in turn led to the rationalisation of a few duplicated goods depots, but relatively little modernisation or significant change was undertaken; for example in 1939 the LMS still had 8,000 horses.

During World War 2, huge quantities of goods were, for a second time, moved by the railways. In 1944 some 500 special trains ran every day for the war effort, but this work once again left the railways exhausted, in a poor state of repair and with war damaged goods facilities. After the war, a glut of cheap war-surplus lorries became available for sale. Flexible pricing to compete with road transport was also prevented by fixed nationally agreed railway charges. These factors resulted in goods being increasingly conveyed by road.

The railways were nationalised in 1948 and inherited over one million goods vehicles of all types. Much of this stock was run down, so new rolling stock began to appear, but with some initially based on old pre-war designs. BR also invested in huge freight marshalling yards for this type of stock. This was at a time when small wagon loads were in sharp decline. There was also an increasing use of block freight trains running directly between one destination and another. All the marshalling yards have since closed down.

Temple Mills Marshalling Yard was one of a number of new freight yards created by BR in the mid-1950s. It had a capacity to handle 100 trains a day, but opened just as wagon-loads were declining and block trains were increasingly used. The main yard closed in 1982 and although much of the wider site has been retained for other railway uses, a derelict section is seen in September 1997. *Author*

There had been a falling off in traditional rail freight since the 1920s and by 1956 more freight was carried by road than rail, but the 1960s and 1970s saw significant further declines in rail freight flows. Even as late as 1965, overnight express freight trains were still being advertised. However, most small stations lost their pick-up goods services in the 1960s and individual small wagon loads ended in the 1970s, their withdrawal resulting in a wholesale loss of business. Fish traffic ceased, to the dismay of many fish merchants, in 1976. Remaining milk traffic ceased in 1981, newspapers in 1988, most parcels in 1999 and most mail trains in 2004, with the closure of the London Post Office Railway the year before.

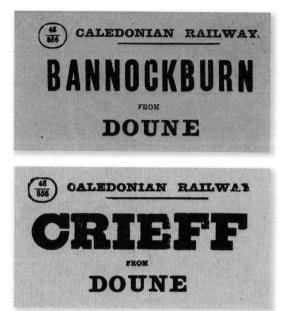

The loss of rail freight has also led to some huge former railway buildings becoming redundant. Imposing examples include the vast GNR goods warehouse in Manchester, once also served by a canal in its depths. The same can be said for both the LNWR goods warehouse at Camden and some of the GNR goods buildings at King's Cross. Large CLC goods sheds are be found at Warrington and Birkenhead and a GCR warehouse at Lincoln. A huge former rail-served whisky warehouse is still extant at Bell Street in Glasgow and a cotton railway warehouse at Stockport. The LNWR Tyndall Street warehouse in Cardiff, the joint LNWR/LYR warehouse at Huddersfield and MR goods buildings at Leicester and Worcester all remain, but there are many other examples. The GNR warehouse at Derby Friargate and the GWR goods depot at Llanelli are hopefully set for future restoration.

Smaller scale and rural goods sheds were built in a huge variety of different designs, but all served a similar function in handling and transferring relatively small and sundry items. Traditional railway goods sheds are now closed, but fortunately the worth of their covered space has often been recognised. As a consequence, hundreds of examples of railway goods sheds have survived in new uses, although demolition endlessly reduces the total. A number of goods sheds on heritage railways are open to the public, whilst some of the larger former goods sheds and warehouses have found new public uses.

The LNER sign at the entrance to Manchester Deansgate Goods Depot in August 2016. The wall and associated terrace of buildings screened the goods yard from adjoining city centre properties. Located close to Central station, tracks once entered the depot on two levels. Use ceased during 1963 and the area has since been transformed into new uses. *Author*

The goods warehouse at Stockport was constructed by the LNWR in 1877. At one time four tracks led into the warehouse. The complete name in white glazed bricks on the building is 'London and North Western Railway Company's Goods Warehouse'. An adjoining engine house once provided hydraulic power to the warehouse lifts and cranes. The building is seen in August 2016. *Author*

Emblazoned on all sides is the 'Great Northern Railway Company's Warehouse' at Manchester. The five-storey fireproof building was completed in 1899 and until 1936 a canal served a basement transhipment dock. As part of the Deansgate Goods Depot, use declined and the building was abandoned in 1963, until it was put to other uses in 1998. It is seen in August 2016. *Author*

The Cheshire Lines Committee Shore Road goods warehouse in Birkenhead seen in September 2006, when it was in use as offices. This was the second largest joint railway and comprised the GNR, GCR and MR, with the aim of trying to break the monopoly of the LNWR in the North West. *Author*

Parcels were once a busy sector of railway goods. Here the ex-GCR parcels office frontage still survives at Leicester Central station. A timetable for perishable parcels on passenger trains was once provided by the GCR. The street-level station buildings remained when this view was taken in September 2016. *Author*

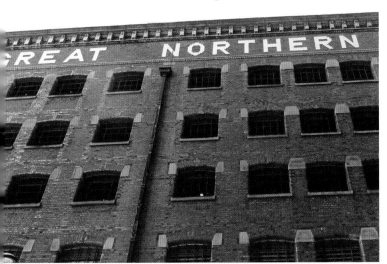

Mildenhall, in Suffolk, possessed an impressive goods shed built by the GER. The functional design with a canopy, sheltering the road loading bays, was widely utilised at goods sheds. The last railway use of this goods shed was in July 1964. The building, seen in September 1993, still remains. *Author*

Holbeach, in Lincolnshire, with a rather utilitarian-looking brick goods shed. The building, dating back to 1858, was closed in May 1965. Seen in August 2009, it has since been demolished. The station would have once been alive with agricultural goods and at peak times freight movements would have taken place until late at night. *Author*

This local sandstone goods shed at Hawes in Yorkshire was sturdily built. Completed in 1878, it was designed in the MR Derby Gothic style and a patterned iron window frame is seen in September 1993. The goods shed was last used for rail freight in April 1964. The building remains and now houses part of the Dales Countryside Museum. *Author*

Almost every goods yard required an office. Here at Crieff, although the LMS as an organisation ceased in 1948 and the goods yard closed in 1967, the derelict office and LMS sign still existed in September 1983 when this view was taken. The site has since been redeveloped. *Author*

*Above:* At King's Cross, a huge goods depot developed to the north of the passenger station. Even when it was being run down in the early 1960s, 25 freight trains a day provided services from all parts of the country. Although many structures have been demolished, some of the best buildings have been retained, such as this former granary store seen in September 2016. *Author*

*Left:* Inside a typical goods shed there could usually be found a loading transhipment platform and a crane, in this case at the East Anglian Railway Museum at Chappel & Wakes Colne in August 1994. The crane came from Saffron Walden, whilst a GER coach, saved from Felixstowe, is seen stored undercover where goods were once transferred between road and rail. *Author*

The local names given to lost lines sometimes provide a clue to the goods once carried. For example, the Derwent Valley Light Railway became known as The Blackberry Line and the GWR route through Cheddar and Wells as The Strawberry Line. The coastal links to Whitstable Harbour and Tollesbury Pier were known as Crab & Winkle lines, whilst the M&SW line through Cricklade was on occasion called The Milky Way. The Shropshire & Montgomeryshire Light Railway was known as The Potts, due to the fact that it used a small part of a much longer proposed line from the Potteries to North Wales. Today the heritage Whisky Line at Elgin and Watercress Line at Alresford signifies their past goods services.

The Spitalfields Goods Depot in East London was once busy with fruit and vegetables and was located to the east of Bishopsgate. A wagon hoist also gave access to the East London Line. Closed in November 1967, much still remained when this view was taken in September 1997. *Author*

The Helen Street disused goods yard and crane at Arbroath, seen in September 2010. The goods shed had been demolished and the yard had been out of use for some time. However, the site next to the main line railway is sensibly safeguarded as a future rail freight facility and trains may yet return. *Author*

Although rail freight is today down from its peak, it is far from dead. In the 1960s it was considered that railways should concentrate on long-distance bulk traffic. The Freightliner concept was recommended in the Beeching Report and services were initiated in the 1960s. Container trains and 100-tonne bogie wagons have been introduced and are just some examples of freight traffic that is still competitively and speedily conveyed by rail. Equally, today much of rail freight is surprisingly transient, with new flows being created and old ones expiring. The consequences are often rusting freight lines and facilities that may well one day spring back into life.

Mistley, in Essex, was the end of the line for this guard's van observed in 1980. The already damaged concrete buffers were never replaced and the goods yard's final use for grain followed in 1985, together with any remaining freight on the Mistley Quay branch the following year. However, some track to the quay remains and future access by rail should perhaps not be discounted. *Author*

# 8
# Lightly filling gaps

By the late 19th century, the railway network had reached almost every centre of importance in the country. However, even little-used rural branch lines had to be built to strict Board of Trade standards and Parliamentary authorisation was required. This raised the prospect of large construction and legal bills, elaborate signalling, fully manned level crossings and raised platforms. The cost of all this meant that some smaller settlements missed out on being connected to the railway network at all.

A number of narrow-gauge lines had been built as these were generally cheaper to construct, together with opportunist standard-gauge branch lines where engineering costs were low. However, it was felt a stimulus was required; thus the Light Railways Act of 1896 was designed to cut red tape and allow local communities to build and run their own railways. It made the prospect of building a railway in the countryside cheaper and easier to run, therefore making it a more attractive commercial proposition for investors. As a consequence of the new legislation, many light railways were proposed to fill in the gaps, and serve remote and often economically depressed parts of the country.

The first railway built under the 1896 Light Railway Act was the 14¼-mile Basingstoke & Alton Light Railway. Opened in June 1901 by the LSWR, few structures survive, but this bridge north of Herriard, seen in July 2016, shows it was not all lightly constructed. Passenger services were ended by the SR in September 1932 and most freight four years later. *Author*

About 60 in total were eventually either opened as new lines, or applied to operate existing lines as light railways under the Act. The Basingstoke & Alton Light Railway was the very first to be sanctioned under the 1896 Act. It was built by the LSWR more to thwart the expansion ambitions of the GWR than to serve the rural communities along its route. It was one of a number operated by main line companies. Most lines had practical purposes and ranged from the Maidens & Dunure in Scotland, built in part to serve the Turnberry Hotel, to the Mid-Suffolk in East Anglia, which served a remote agricultural area.

There was special charm in the light railways managed by Colonel Stephens. He was closely associated with the construction and operation of some 16 light railways, including the Kent & East Sussex. He ran his light railway empire with ingenuity and economy from his headquarters, a terraced house in Tonbridge. Mixed trains, second-hand equipment and the innovative early use of petrol-driven rail cars all featured on his distinctive railways.

The station buildings on many light railways were often far removed from some of the substantial buildings of the main line railways. The invention of corrugated iron, which in the 1900s had become rust proofed by the use of

Alton Park station was provided for a hospital and college by a siding from the light railway. It was also sometimes unkindly known as the Cripples' Home siding. The station, which was not advertised in public timetables, was served by special trains until 1939. Coal was also delivered to the siding and this traffic survived until November 1967. The concrete platform is seen in July 2016. *N. Day*

Fallgate station building in Derbyshire, of corrugated iron construction, was typical of the 7½-mile Ashover Light Railway narrow-gauge practice. The building remained in June 1999 and still survives. Regular passenger services ceased in September 1930, although summer services were run until 1936, special trains until 1947 and freight until March 1950. *Author*

Where standard-gauge was used, several new lines were built by simply following the contours of the land to avoid unnecessary gradients and costly engineering works. This often resulted in stations being some considerable way from the village or town they served. Lightly laid track, ungated crossings, sharp curves and modest bridges often resulted in speeds being slow. Passenger trains were frequently mixed with freight and these were limited to 25mph by other legislation.

*Above:* The 19-mile Mid-Suffolk Light Railway provided corrugated iron station buildings. Such buildings were sometimes found on light railways and a few still survive on their original sites. Equally, instances of those originally on the MSLR are also to be found, such as that from Laxfield located at Mangapps Railway Museum in August 2012. *Author*

*Left:* The Mid-Suffolk Light Railway closed in July 1952, but a short section has been reopened as a heritage line. Brockford station is seen here, with a quiet period in August 2013. The locomotive, *Wissington*, is a 1938-built 0-6-0ST and was used on the ex-sugar beet factory network of lines of that name in Norfolk. *Author*

galvanising and stronger from being made from mild steel, transformed the economics of building. Kits could be constructed without great skills, reduced heavy transport costs and were surprisingly durable. Thus, it became a building material of choice for a number of light railways.

Although most light railways were, as the name suggests, lightly built, there were equally some built with significant engineering features. This includes the concrete viaducts on the Lyme Regis and Wanlockhead branches, although the latter has been demolished.

The 19½-mile main route of the Axholme Joint Railway was a joint venture by the LYR and NER, that took over the Goole & Marshland Light Railway and the Axholme Light Railway. A viaduct over drainage channels on the line is seen in August 2008. The eight arches were all numbered at their crown with cast iron plates. Closure of the final section came in April 1965. *Author*

Where the terrain was difficult, narrow-gauge railways came into their own as they were cheaper and more flexible to build. Amongst the narrow-gauge passenger lines promoted by the Light Railway Act were the Ashover, Sand Hutton, Leek & Manifold, Vale of Rheidol, Welsh Highland, Welshpool & Llanfair and Campbeltown & Machrihanish. Even the Southwold Railway took advantage of the Act for its short harbour extension. The Ffestiniog Railway had long been open and had little light railway atmosphere, but obtained a light railway order to economise on certain aspects of its operation.

The 5½-mile Elsenham & Thaxted Light Railway provided an impressive water tower and engine shed at Thaxted, Cambridge sub-shed 31A, seen in March 2012. Closed in June 1953, the wooden passenger terminus also survives here. The station at Thaxted was located some way from town to save on construction costs. *Author*

The 8¼-mile Southwold Railway used the Light Railway Act for its 1-mile harbour branch. This struck off from the narrow-gauge main line near the swing bridge and closed with the rest of the railway in April 1929. Remains of the bridge over the River Blyth, which was originally required by the Harbour Commissioners to have a swing section, are seen in June 1999. *Author*

The 6-mile Campbeltown & Machrihanish Light Railway originated in 1876 as a colliery line, but was upgraded in 1906 and opened as a narrow-gauge passenger light railway. Closed in November 1932, the former trackbed, on a 1 in 35 rising gradient, from the quayside at Campbeltown, is now used as a footpath and is seen in September 1999. *Author*

Most of the proposed light railways were not built, which in some ways was fortunate as the Act could not save lines from the inevitable as road competition grew. The feeble finances of many narrow-gauge light railways, which required the transhipment of freight, also resulted in some relatively early closures. The Campbeltown & Machrihanish closed in November 1931, the Sand Hutton in June 1932 and the Leek & Manifold was closed by the LMS in March 1934. The Welsh Highland closed in May 1937, although the GWR kept the Welshpool & Llanfair line open for freight and reopened the Vale of Rheidol in 1945. The remaining slate trains on the Ffestiniog ceased the following year. Freight on the Ashover Light Railway survived until March 1950 and the Welshpool & Llanfair until November 1956.

On the standard-gauge light railways some closures began in the 1930s, whilst several lines closed to passengers during World War 2, never to see these services restored, such as the Cairn Valley and most of the Maidens & Dunure light railways. The Weston, Clevedon & Portishead, Wick & Lybster and Leadhills & Wanlockhead light railways never reopened at all after the war. Of those light railways that continued into the BR era many were killed off relatively early, although some survived until the mid-1960s.

Timetables from 1932

Of the narrow-gauge light railways, the Vale of Rheidol was reprieved from BR closure, whilst the Ffestiniog and Welsh Highland Railway routes are reopened, together with the Welshpool & Llanfair. Of the original standard-gauge light railways, although very few still remain in use, the heritage Kent & East Sussex is reopened for much of its route, whilst the East Kent, Leadhills & Wanlockhead and Mid-Suffolk also have reopened heritage sections.

The 5-mile Rothesay & Ettrick Bay Light Railway was a narrow-gauge, mostly roadside tramway, running a fleet of electric tramcars on the Isle of Bute. Consent for the line had been obtained under a wide interpretation of the Light Railways Act. The tramway closed in September 1936. At Port Bannatyne the tram depot still survives as a bus garage and is seen in June 2016. *Dr A. Grundy*

# 9
# Fortunes of the Big Four

The government took control of the railways during World War 1 and only relinquished control in 1921. A few local lines were closed, whilst the completion of railway projects was put on hold. The railway finances of many railway companies were weakened by the war effort, but lessons were learnt during this period. It was decided that by building on this experience the railways would be more efficient if most of the hundred or so disparate railway companies were grouped into just four big railway companies.

The 'Big Four' was the name popularly given to the newly created four large railway companies. The London Midland & Scottish Railway (LMS) was the largest, the London & North Eastern Railway (LNER) was the second largest, the Great Western Railway (GWR), benefited from continuity and the Southern Railway (SR) was the smallest. The four came into being in 1923 and the names broadly reflected the geographical areas that they served.

Such large changes had the potential to cause difficulties, but the new companies were often slow in consolidating their constituents; many changes came gradually and unnecessary costs were avoided. The permanence of the pre-Grouping companies was often reflected by their maps, sometimes produced on tiles or on enamel. These were mostly retained by the Big Four, together with other equipment embossed or marked with the pre-Grouping companies' crests or initials, until such time as it needed replacement. Much survived into BR days.

The Big Four made quite differing attempts to feature parts of the pre-Grouping coats of arms into their own new crests, except the GWR which, of course, remained the same. However, in the 1930s creeping modernisation resulted in more symbolism and some slicker logos were introduced, particularly on main lines and on notice boards. In the lead were the LNER with their corporate approach introduced by their marketing department. The Art Deco and consistent lettering was very distinctive and modern. The LMS, more than any of the others, eventually introduced standardisation, the Southern

The LMS covered large parts of the country. The slightly unwieldly company covered nearly 40% of the total route miles and was the largest of the Big Four companies, once employing some 250,000 persons. The map dates from 1946.

highlighted its electrification programme, whilst the distinctive GWR monogram was introduced and publicity stressed the speed of their main line services.

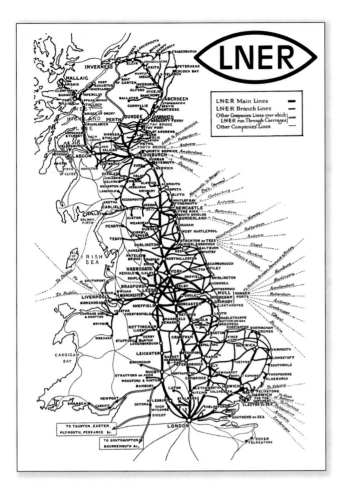

The LNER was the least profitable of the Big Four. It had the second largest route miles of about 6,500 and included most of the country east of the Pennines, together with East Anglia. The map dates from 1930.

SR green decoration at Southampton Terminus in November 1995. The SR was the smallest of the Big Four, with over 2,000 route miles. It served the south of England from Kent to tentacles in Cornwall. It was noted for its extensive passenger electrification programme. Non-electrified lines later became targets for closure. *Author*

GWR enamel map, dated around 1906, when Fishguard Harbour opened. As its name suggests, it served the west of England south of Birkenhead. With about 3,800 route miles, it provided services to Ireland and its lines in South Wales once carried huge amounts of coal. *Author*

GWR crest at Birmingham Snow Hill in August 2001, dating from the rebuilding of the station between 1906–1912. The GWR was the only railway to retain its original name in 1923. The GWR, with a few hiccups, paid a dividend to its shareholders until it was nationalised. Its corporate image survived well into BR days. *Author*

The General Strike of 1926 had led to a little traffic being lost to the roads, but it was the years of the Great Depression, starting in 1929, that took a toll on the Big Four's finances. The LMS closed Barrow-in-Furnace and Stoke-on-Trent locomotive works in 1930. The LNER, the least profitable, with others cut the wages of staff for a while and effectively closed Melton Constable works in 1936. The GWR drew on reserves and downgraded many stations to unstaffed halts.

A blue LNER enamel bill board top at the heritage Mid-Suffolk Light Railway in August 2013. Blue was widely used by the LNER for such signs in East Anglia, in some ways perpetuating the colours of the GER. A rather different Garter Blue livery was used for some express locomotives designed by Sir Nigel Gresley. *Author*

There were also consequences of the economic depression for the railway network and a number of lines had their passenger services withdrawn by the Big Four. Cuts were mostly on the lightest-used rural lines, but the extent can be judged from the examples below. The LNER in 1930 withdrew services on Alnwick–Coldstream, Dalmeny–Ratho and Allendale–Hexham routes, together with lines around Bathgate. Bourne–Sleaford, Stoke Ferry–Denver and the Cawood–Selby lines were also closed to passengers in the same year. Passenger services on the Aberthaw–Cowbridge, Rhymney–New Tredegar, Bridport–West Bay and Drybook–Bilson lines were all withdrawn by the GWR in 1930. The Airdrie–Newhouse, Bonnybridge–Greenhill, Denny–Larbert, Holytown–Morningside and Kilbirnie–Giffen were all routes closed to passengers in Scotland by the LMS in 1930. Elsewhere, the Aldridge–Brownhills, Mansfield–Staveley, Ripley–Derby, Normanton–Ashby-de-la-Zouch and Glasson Dock lines had passenger services terminated by the LMS in 1930. Meanwhile, the SR withdrew passenger services, including those on the Tooting Junction–Merton Park line in 1929, the Hythe–Sandgate, Canterbury–Whitstable and Lee-on-Solent–Fort Brockhurst lines in 1931, the Alton–Basingstoke line in 1932 and the Ringwood–Christchurch line in 1933.

The Big Four also cut services on their narrow-gauge lines at this time. The LNER would not help the independent Southwold Railway survive in 1929. The LMS closed the Leek & Manifold line to all traffic in 1934 and the SR closed the Lynton & Barnstaple Railway to all traffic in 1935. The GWR closed passenger services on the Corris and Welshpool lines in 1931, but freight did survive here and on their other narrow-gauge lines.

*Below:* A SR handbill announcing the closure of the narrow-gauge Lynton & Barnstaple Railway on 30 September 1935. Rarely had the closing of a line resulted in such upset and a large crowd braved rain to say goodbye to the iconic line. Its reopening is the last great piece of railway preservation business.
*NRM/Science & Society Picture Library*

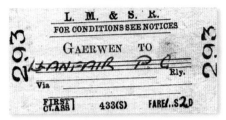

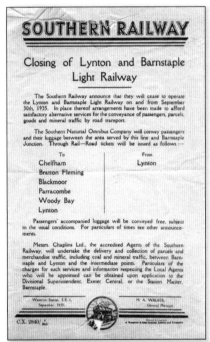

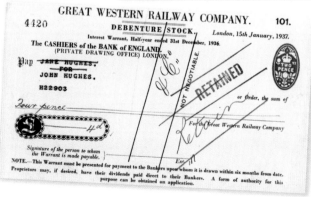

Ever more disturbing events in Europe led to preparations for war being started by the Big Four in 1937. When war was declared once again in 1939, the railways came under government control with the Railway Executive Committee being established, as had been the case during World War 1. The Big Four transported troops involved in the evacuation of Dunkirk, they were severely damaged by enemy bombings, but were to go on and facilitate the D-Day re-entry of Allied forces into France. In fact, during World War 2, the Big Four provided the greatest achievement in railway transport the world has ever known. They stepped up output by 46%, while 25% of workshop capacity was diverted to the war effort and 15% of the staff released for other war duties.

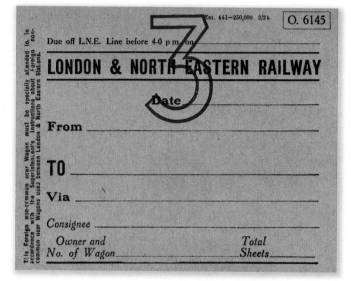

Over 1,000 miles of line had been closed by the Big Four prior to 1939. During World War 2, many stations had their services disrupted, slowed and cut back, whilst a range of mostly short and less-used lines were closed to passengers either at the start or during the war. These included Strathaven–Darvel, Douglas West–Brocketsbrae, Loch Tay–Killin, the Turnberry line, Angel Road–Lower Edmonton, Edgware–Finchley Church End, Port Clarence–Billingham-on-Tees, Blackhill–Durham, Bottesford–Newark, Stafford–Uttoxeter, Beighton–Shirebrook, Eddington Junction–Derby, Langwith Junction–Beighton, Maldon–Woodham Ferrers, Forncett–Wymondham and The Devil's Dyke branch. When hostilities ceased the Big Four were reluctant to reopen many of these lines to passengers and many were quietly left to slip into oblivion.

Bomb damage closed the Addison Road–North Acton line in 1940 and the Stratford Low Level–Victoria Park service in 1942. Damage to other stations caused some premature and what turned out to be permanent or long-term passenger closures, ranging from the Gallions and Beckton lines in London docklands to Gorleston North station in Norfolk. Locomotives, freight depots and rolling stock were destroyed; railwaymen worked long hours. There were acts of great courage; for example two footplate staff moving a burning ammunition train from Soham received the George Cross, whilst the LMS alone lost some 1,500 employees on active service.

Throughout World War 2, the railways had been intensively used once again, but with minimum maintenance and renewal. Subsequently, the Big Four were run down at the end of the war and much of their stock and track was worn out, even more so than was the case after World War 1. Nationalisation came in 1948 and a single British Railways was formed with regions broadly reflecting the former Big Four.

# 10
# Clever use of concrete

The artificial stone called concrete became increasingly popular for railway construction. The viaduct on the closed Killin branch over the River Dochart, dating from 1886, uses both concrete and stone. The first concrete sleeper can be traced back to 1884.

Sir Robert McAlpine, known as 'Concrete Bob', was a pioneer in the use of concrete. The Glenfinnan Viaduct in Scotland, completed in 1898, is one of his greatest achievements. It remains in use, together with many more of his concrete railway structures. On lines that are closed, his firm was involved with the mass concrete viaduct built in 1901 at Risping Cleugh on the Wanlockhead branch. Built in a traditional arched style it was unusually clad with terracotta bricks. After closure in 1938 and years of neglect some of the brick covering became loose and very reluctantly it was decided to demolish the viaduct by explosives in 1991.

Concrete is a somewhat uncompromising grey material to work with; consequently Sir Robert McAlpine innovatively developed a technique to colour the face of his concrete, to the depth of about an inch, with a reddish hue. Horizontal lines were also scored on some surfaces. This gave a very successful impression that local red sandstone blocks had been used in the work. The coloured concrete also blended in well with brickwork and the landscape and was used at a number of locations.

At Fort Augustus in Scotland, the railway to the Pier station involved the construction of a 300ft (91m) viaduct consisting of steel lattice girders supported by castellated concrete columns, embellished with crosses. This section of line closed to regular passenger trains in September 1906, but the concrete support remains of the bridge are seen in June 2010. *Author*

Concrete used at the ex-CR Bowling station, which opened in 1896 and closed in February 1951, was produced to an attractive reddish hue by Sir Robert McAlpine, with the use of iron oxide as an outer layer colourant. A section of the unusual coloured concrete platform edge is seen here at Fawley Hill in Oxfordshire, the home of Sir William McAlpine, in April 2016. *Author*

Such was his success that railway bridges and viaducts on closed lines in the Scotland were also constructed in concrete by other contractors, the first time this material had been used on a large scale for such purposes. Fortunately, many concrete structures remain on closed lines such as those on the Fort Augustus and St Fillans lines, as their demolition can be difficult and the scrap value is negligible.

The use of concrete was also pioneered by William Marriott at Melton Constable Works on the M&GN. He found concrete to be an excellent substitute for brick, wood and steel which were all in short supply, particularly during the period around World War 1. He extensively introduced concrete fencing posts in 1909 and lightweight sleepers in 1916. Growing housing development and the new Norwich ring road necessitated the construction of two new bridges over the line, north of Norwich City station. The bridges were mostly built of concrete blocks with steel beams encased in concrete, opening in 1923.

Melton Constable supplied other railways and the GNR was a big customer of concrete signal posts. The curing of concrete is a skilled job and concrete products were manufactured up until 1936 when the concrete works were closed by the LNER. Examples of concrete fence posts, mileposts and name boards made by the works still survive, demonstrating their clever manufacture which in turn resulted in their durability.

Fort Augustus Pier station in June 2010. The gap in the concrete quay allowed livestock to enter the holds of ships. Built to main line standards, passenger trains were originally intended to connect here with steamboat services along Loch Ness to Inverness. Freight to the Pier station was discontinued by the LNER in July 1924. *Author*

The Fort Augustus–Spean Bridge branch opened in 1903. Many of the civil engineering structures on the line were built in concrete to high specifications and remain in good condition. A concrete skew-arch bridge spans a spur tow path from the Caledonian Canal at Fort Augustus and is seen in June 2010. *Author*

A weathered retaining wall at St Fillans station in Scotland dating from 1904. Large concrete structures were sometimes provided with parallel scoring to break up the plain surface. The ex-CR station closed to passengers in October 1951, although track remained until 1959 and the view of the station approach is seen here in June 2004. *Author*

*Above:* The Gedney station sign in Lincolnshire was moulded in different coloured concretes at the M&GN Melton Constable Works, prior to the closure of the concrete making section in 1936. It is an amazing survivor; the station closed to passengers in February 1959 and this view was taken at the derelict site in November 2009. *Author*

*Right:* A preserved M&GN concrete milepost at Winchcombe Museum. The company initials only appeared on the full mileposts and not on the sub-divided quarter mileposts. The early days of concrete were one of experimentation and on one railway the first hard frost reduced all the new concrete mileposts to piles of sand and cement. *Author*

*Opposite:* The concrete viaduct spanning Ogle Burn at Lochearnhead is seen in June 2004. There are seven 40ft (12m) spans and two half-spans at each end. The design includes channelling and headstone effects moulded into the concrete to imitate stone designs. The viaduct dates from 1904 and weathering for over a century has caused some staining. *Author*

A concrete bridge at Barnard Avenue, north of Yarmouth Beach station. It was part of a scheme implemented by the LNER before World War 2 to improve operations on this once busy section. The line was one of the first major closures by BR in February 1959, but the bridge remains and is seen in November 2012. *Author*

The LSWR had established a concrete factory at Exmouth Junction. The SR realised the potential of concrete, from bridges to smaller items, to reduce maintenance costs and the works were expanded in the mid-1920s. Some of the familiar precast and reinforced concrete designs date from this time, but patterns changed and a number of concrete products were only used for a few years.

There were different forms of concrete station name boards and different designs of reinforced concrete footbridge, before a more standard design was developed. The well-known SR permanent way and fogman's huts, concrete platforms, distinctive concrete wall panels, palings and fence posts were all poured out. Concrete products that could not fit within the loading gauge often came as 'flat packs' to be assembled on site and fixed-length sections could be used in multiples for any length of platform.

A modern bridge was built over the Canterbury & Whitstable Railway in 1923, to convey the Thanet Way highway. The use of green pigment concrete decoration would have reflected SR colours. The large bridge is pictured in May 1995. It was quite a comparison to the small bridges on the original line. *Author*

The SR concrete station lamp post, seen here within the trees, was one of a number of designs. The plain concrete name board allowed an enamel sign to be affixed to the face. This is at Horam in Sussex, now part of the Cuckoo Trail, and is seen here in April 1995. These concrete items and concrete platform are all that remain of the original station. *Author*

Throughout the former SR area, examples of concrete products survive on closed routes, many still in good condition. Smaller scale products include trackside huts, station name boards, uniquely topped concrete gate posts, fencing posts, distinctive lamp post brackets, mileage and gradient posts and many more can still be found. Numerous concrete drainage culverts and cable ducts also remain, whilst some concrete telegraph posts and sleepers could be discovered on the Lynton & Barnstaple Railway long after closure.

The SR concrete sign at Egloskerry was still *in situ* in September 1995. The Launceston–Padstow line was part of the 'withered arm' of SR lines in the South West. The station closed in October 1966; the concrete sign would have been made at the SR's Exmouth Junction Concrete Works. *Author*

The SR gate post with a typical flamboyant concrete finial at Lydford station in Devon in September 1995. The finial would have fitted over the top of a standard concrete post. Considerable skill was required in constructing the concrete moulds and ensuring the quality and curing of the concrete. *Author*

The concrete Cannington Viaduct on the Lyme Regis branch suffered subsidence, which was stabilised by an additional brick diaphragm and arch. Problems with the 92ft (28m) high structure delayed opening of the branch and added to costs. Trains ceased to use the viaduct in November 1965 and this view was taken September 1995. *Author*

A SR concrete gradient post on the route to Padstow near Egloskerry in September 1995. The figures have been painted black; on other sections of the SR different colour schemes were applied, with white numerals on a green background also being used. The rising arm with 330 indicates 1ft of ascent for every 330ft length of track. *Author*

The SR built a number of concrete stations, but the largest concrete structure designed by the SR was the Ocean Terminal at Southampton Docks. The Art Deco ultra-modern building was intended to surpass any airline terminal at that time. Completion was delayed by World War 2, but by the time of opening in 1950 the jet airliner was killing off ocean liner traffic. The terminal was closed at the end of 1980 and the substantial concrete building was later demolished, with some difficulty.

Of the other Big Four railways, they all used concrete for bridges, sleepers, fencing, cable troughs, platforms and numerous other ancillary railway uses. The GWR established a concrete works at Taunton in the 1900s. They made a comprehensive range of products and dedicated railway wagons were dispatched from the works. The GWR also commissioned a large concrete goods shed at Canon's Marsh at Bristol and used concrete for a number of other buildings. The LMS moved the engineers responsible for the concrete Greenisland Viaducts in Ireland to London in the 1930s and between 1936–39 opened a number of new concrete stations. They also established a concrete depot at Newton Heath during World War 2 and made prestressed concrete beams, in particular for war damaged bridges. The LNER once had concrete depots at York and, after closure of Melton Constable, at Lowestoft producing sleepers and a range of products. On a small scale, the LNER provided a concrete permanent way hut which could be assembled from quite small sections. On a large-scale concrete was particularly used by the LNER for locomotive coaling towers.

Southampton Docks with the remains of the Ocean Terminal. The Art Deco concrete terminal was designed by the SR, but only completed in July 1950 due to the delay of World War 2, by which time the use of ocean liners was in sharp decline. The well-built concrete building was mostly demolished in 1983, but the last concrete remains, pictured in August 2013, were removed in 2014. *Author*

A wide variety of concrete products continued to be produced by BR, but the traditional territories of the concrete works were disregarded and some Exmouth Junction products ended up as far as Wales and Humberside. However, BR required less concrete and closed Exmouth Junction Works in 1963 and Taunton Works in 1995. The railways still make extensive use of concrete and concrete sleepers are now in almost universal usage.

The GWR Cardiff station water tower was completed in 1932 and located on the old fish-dock platform; it is viewed in September 2010. Many GWR concrete products can still be found throughout the network, even today. A huge traditionally built water tower was also provided at the nearby Canton engine shed. *Author*

Form follows function as seen with this BR 1950s concrete footbridge at Highbridge station in Somerset, in March 2009. The pre-cast construction of the reinforced components allowed for much flexibility. The link to the closed S&D platforms has been removed and the entire bridge has since been demolished. *Author*

Here at Dunford Bridge on the east side of Woodhead Tunnel, BR era concrete lamp posts were still to be found in September 1994. As to the tunnel itself, at least a 21in thickness of concrete was used for the lining. Sadly, the route through here and the tunnel closed in July 1981. *Author*

# British Railways

The Big Four railways were run down and financially damaged by the herculean task they performed during World War 2. These problems, combined with a policy to nationalise public services at the time, saw the creation of the British Transport Commission and in turn the establishment of British Railways in 1948. The new BR divided the country into six distinct regions, broadly coinciding with the earlier Big Four railways, but creating separate regions for Scotland, the East and the North East. The new regions were issued with totem-shaped enamel station nameplates. Each region had its own distinctive colour scheme that was reflected in these and other station signs.

The Scottish Region encompassed the ex-LNER and LMS lines in Scotland. The region adopted a light blue house colour for enamel station signs and publications, not dissimilar to the livery of the Caledonian Railway locomotives. The headquarters were based at Buchanan Street in Glasgow.

BR map 1949, showing about 20,000 miles of line.

The Scottish Region used an attractive light sky blue as the regional colour for signs and timetables. Edinburgh Princes Street station sign is seen in September 1965, just a few days before closure. The train shed was subsequently demolished, but the hotel remains. *Author*

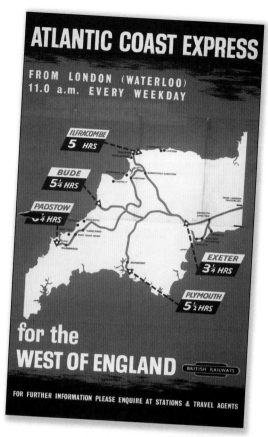

The London Midland Region used a maroon colour, similar to the LMS locomotive livery, for signs and publications. The General Manager was based at Euston, but later moved to Birmingham. Many ex-LMS lines in South Wales were transferred to the WR. From 1956 maroon liveried coaches were widely introduced on all regions.

The North Eastern Region used a colourful orange or tangerine for signs and publications. The headquarters were based at York, whilst shipping services from Hull and Middlesbrough to the rest of the world were included on its maps. In 1967 it was merged with the Eastern Region, although some offices were retained in York.

The Eastern Region used a dark blue, similar to the livery of GER locomotives. New signs on the ex-GER, ex-LTSR and ex-GNR stations were all in this blue. However, at one time its maps used the dark blue for the ex-GER lines, brown for ex-LTSR lines and green for the ex-GNR lines. The General Manager was based at Liverpool Street Station. At Lowestoft Central a huge dark blue BR enamel sign delightfully remained in 2017.

The Western Region, after trailing black and white, used brown and cream colours. The region lost some ex-GWR lines west of Birmingham which were transferred to the LMR, but in 1958 annexed ex-SR lines west of Exeter and the ex-S&D. The headquarters were based at Paddington. The WR reintroduced a chocolate and cream livery of the GWR on their coaches for a time.

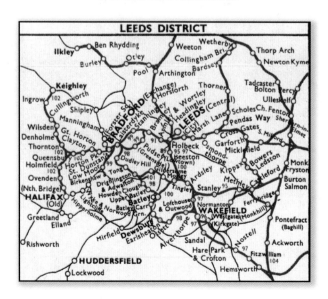

North Eastern Region Leeds inset map 1948. The LMR Oxenhope branch is not shown.

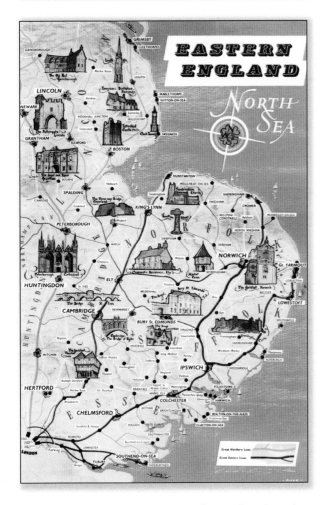

*Above:* Many of the black and white signs of the GWR were repainted by BR in chocolate and cream. The cost of replacing GWR cast iron signs would have been prohibitive so innovation in painting was sometimes used as this sign on the heritage Gwili Railway in October 2002 demonstrates. *Author*

*Above:* BR Eastern Region map of 1965 showing places of interest. Similar illustrated maps were produced for other areas.

*Below:* The Southern Region perpetuated green for their coaches, signs and most publications. This rather unusual enamel sign was to be found at Barnstaple Town station in 1995 and still survives. It should perhaps just be noted that after the station closed in October 1970 all signs were removed from the buildings. *Author*

# HAWKHURST

The Southern Region soon broadly followed the green coloured themes of the Southern Railway and a darker green ultimately continued to be used on passenger coaches. The General Manager was based at Waterloo and, until some areas in the South West were taken over by the Western Region, it very much covered the same area as the Southern Railway.

BR was in some ways unfortunate in that it was the custodian of Britain's railways at a time when they went into sharp decline. The pictures of filthy steam engines and run-down gas-lit stations were not good images in the 'swinging sixties'. Its curled-up sandwiches became a national joke, but this all belied an industry that had to cope with massive decline and change. From 1965 it traded under the title of British Rail and a corporate Rail Blue livery was used for the stock of all regions.

Class D16/3 4-4-0 No 62517, dating from 1901, at Caister in July 1957 on the ex-M&GN line to Yarmouth Beach. It is clear from this view that the signalling and locomotive all required renewal. The alternative to modernisation was closure and this line closed less than two years later, the first major closure by BR. The locomotive was scrapped at the same time. *Colour-Rail E713 E. Alger*

Southwell station in April 1959, with a MR Johnson 0-6-0T No 58065 in charge of the push-pull service to Rolleston Junction. Many such branches had seen little investment and as with this line were early candidates for closure by BR. Passenger services ceased at Southwell in June 1959, although freight survived until May 1966. *Colour-Rail M707 D. H. Beecroft*

Trains cross on the single ex-GWR line at Lampeter in July 1964 on the Carmarthen–Aberystwyth line, which closed in February 1965 due in part to the cost of repairing flood damage. The approaching 'Manor' class 4-6-0 No 7826 *Longworth Manor* is seen here and was itself scrapped in 1965. There have been calls for the line to be reopened. *Colour-Rail W1182 A. B. Jeffrey*

To accompany the Modernisation Plan, in 1956 BR began to introduce a new crest, with what was sometimes unkindly known as 'the ferret and dartboard'. The emblem is viewed in June 2009 from a BR Mark 1 Pullman coach on the heritage West Somerset Railway. *Author*

As it turned out, BR developed a somewhat dogmatic and inflexible attitude to running railways. Operating costs were allowed to get out of control; everything seemed to be calculated to ensure ultimately there would be no alternative to closure. By way of example, the LMR for a time refused to introduce unstaffed stations, bizarrely suggesting the only saving would be wages. Tracks were renewed just before closure, new bridges constructed just before closure, such as north of Sudbury. Woodbridge signal box was decommissioned, then repainted and then demolished.

A 'Brighton Belle' coach in the Rail Blue and grey BR livery that was applied to corridor stock from 1965, including the Pullman cars from 1969. They were withdrawn in April 1972 and some are seen in store at Stewarts Lane in April 1988. The London–Brighton train started in 1933 and was the world's only electric all-Pullman express. *Author*

Although passenger services to Tongwynlais ceased in July 1931, a DMU is seen here at Coryton, the cut-back terminus of the line. This was August 1963 and it was Driver Haigist's last few shifts before retirement. The author once lived near here as a child and walked the 'rusty line' to the nearby, but now long-demolished, Melingriffith Tin Works. *Author*

British Railways became British Rail in 1965 and the double-arrow logo was established. Croxley Green station is seen displaying the sign in September 1997. The electric railway link to this station was severed 'temporarily' by a new road in March 1966. A new railway bridge over the new road was never constructed and the station closed formally in September 2003. *Author*

BR introduced a range of diesel locomotives to replace steam. Here a Type 4 'Warship' diesel-hydraulic locomotive, D828 *Magnificent*, is seen at Bath Green Park in February 1966, having hauled a special train. Green Park closed the following month and it is said prejudice against diesel-hydraulic 'non-standard' engines saw this entire class withdrawn by 1972. *Colour-Rail DE1832 R. Leitch*

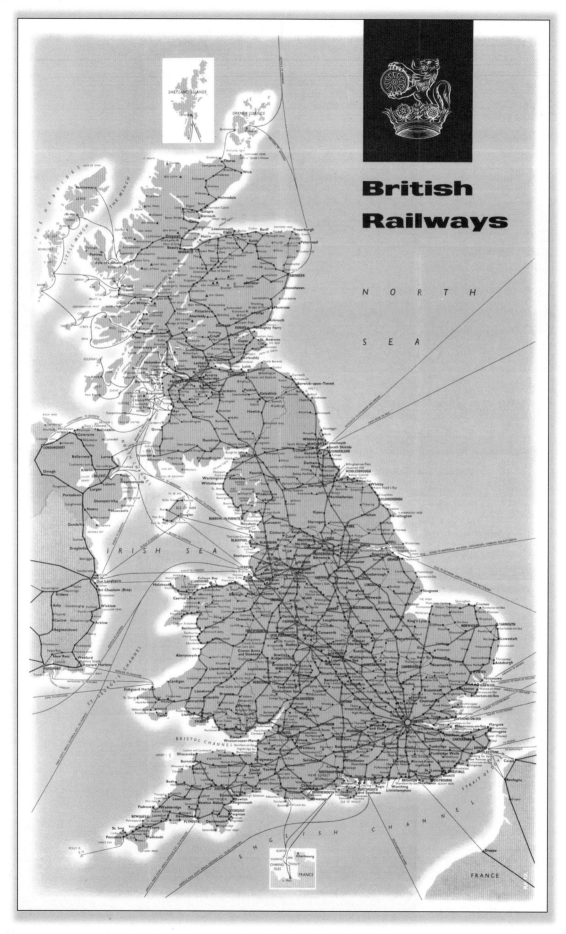

BR map 1960, between 1955 and 1958, about 80 branch lines and 350 stations were closed.

BR suffered from strikes, in some cases to continue outdated working practices. Yet being in the public sector, wages remained low, including those of management. When Dr Beeching arrived from the private sector, the existing railway board and the unions mostly went along with his plan, even though he had no railway expertise and they did. Management on some occasions seemed hell bent on taking the least line of resistance. It was more in keeping with the Chairman's policy to close a line than work hard and innovatively to keep it open.

However, a turnaround was eventually achieved. With the introduction of the Inter City 125 train and electrification of the WCML passenger numbers started to increase and BR became a world leader in high-speed travel. It also became the second most efficient railway in Europe. This all helped to prevent further closures. By 1992 the regions had been replaced by business sectors. Such was BR's later success that the endless political football of railways was kicked back into privatisation, beginning in 1994.

Overall, the period of nationalisation under BR in the 1960s resulted in a large number of closures, causing damage to the railways. It is not the intention of this book to pass judgement on different political approaches to the railways and you will see elsewhere that I am also critical of the current situation. However, whatever your view, passenger numbers have doubled since privatisation and more lines have reopened than closed.

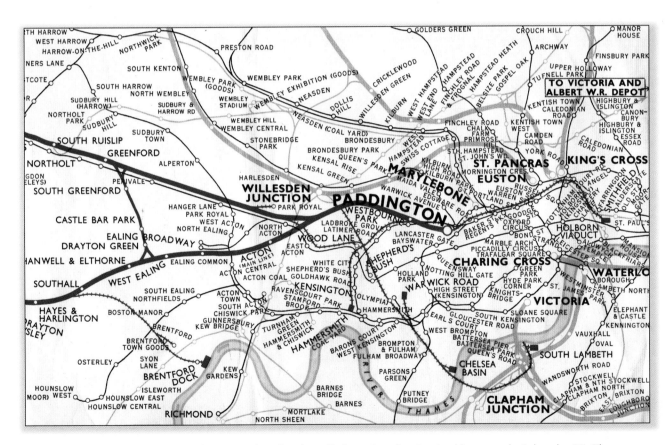

WR map of the London area in the 1960s showing how little rationalisation had been undertaken by BR. The map would not have been much different in 1923.

# 12

# Beeching's biggest blunders

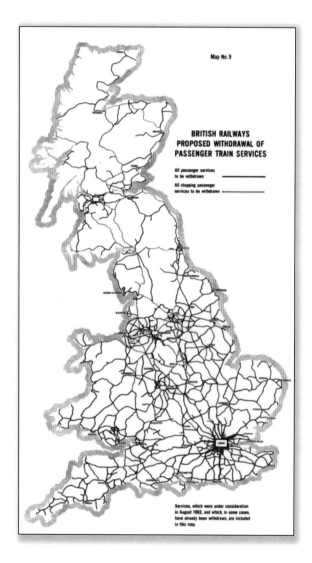

The 1963 Beeching Report map of proposed closures. The preciseness was based on unsound statistics. It was also odd that some lines out of London showed density of passenger traffic.

By 1955, increasing financial losses were recorded by BR and the Modernisation Plan was produced with a policy for steam to be replaced by diesel and electric traction, together with the creation of vast new freight marshalling yards. The plan was designed to reduce the deficit, but did little to stem pre-war working practices, including 'common carrier' legal requirements, which allowed road haulage to pick lucrative freight and leave the railways with the often unprofitable residue. As passengers and freight traffic increasingly shifted to the roads, the losses increased. The Branch Lines Committee had also been set up to close the least used lines and about 200 branches and secondary routes had already been closed by 1962.

The failure of the Modernisation Plan and earlier closures to cut losses led in 1963 to the Reshaping of British Railways report that recommended mass closure of the railway network in Britain, including over 2,300 stations and about 5,000 miles of line. The recommendations included closing all lines north of Inverness and on the Isle of Wight. Large areas of rural Scotland, Wales, the South West and East Coast would also be left without any railways. It was known as the Beeching Report because Dr Richard Beeching was its instigator. He was the Chairman, of what in 1963 became the British Railways Board, with an objective to force the railways into an economically sounder position.

The Beeching Report was unpopular and when Dr Beeching was kicked by a railway man, I was delighted. I am going to give him my own kicking now. In my view, he was a somewhat arrogant person whose own high opinion of himself disguised a basic lack of understanding of railway economics. No real attempt was made to attract more custom. There was no flexibility to allow marginal loss-making lines to be retained rather than closed. No attempt was made to protect routes for possible future reopening.

The sole intention of the single vision and inflexible report was to justify its pre-conceived conclusions. The

# BEECHING'S NEXT RAILWAY "CURE"

## Says Trunk Route Plan Could Save Up To £100m

### STRESSES NEED FOR EARLY DECISION

Dr. Beeching, talking to a Press conference yesterday about the plan for rationalisation—the second stage in his "cure" for British Railways—said it would be reasonable to assume that the net saving could be between £50 million and £100 million a year when the plan had been carried out.

He said there could be a "major controversy" over the plan, but the unions were not displeased with it.

**He disclosed that the Minister of Transport had had the report of the plan for "quite a time," but he would not discuss the Minister's opinion on it, which, Dr. Beeching said, had been expressed to him in private.**

"I am quite satisfied with his opinion," Dr. Beeching added. Asked if there were dates other than 1984 for completion of rationalisation of the railways, he replied that no dates had been thought of.

But it was his hope, and that of the people responsible for carrying it out, that an agreed decision about the railways would be reached as soon as possible "so we can take action and put our house in order as fast as possible."

The report on the plan, which foresees hundreds of giant trains hurtling non-stop over a streamlined network of trunk routes connecting the main centres, says the train can both compete with and complement the car, the road freighter and the aeroplane.

The aim would be to concentrate on bulk transport over routes of heavy demand, cutting trunk ways to an effective 3,000 miles, instead of the present 7,500 miles which connect the main centres.

Stopping services on the trunk routes are seen to be uneconomical and the 2,100 trains a day which are envisaged will be through trains.

### *Blue-print For 1984*

The report, "The Development of the Major Trunk Routes," does not deal with commuter services. These are being specially considered. It is a blue print for 1984, 20 years being taken as the limit of a realistic survey.

The second stage has different intentions from Dr. Beeching's first plan, published in 1963, which was designed to cut out the unsound and uneconomic parts of the rail system. The report points out that it is "not a prelude to closures on a grand scale," but is the basis for better planning.

"The danger is that failure to change, to modernise and to concentrate will cause the present decline to continue," it warns.

# RAIL CLOSURES: 21 MORE TO GO

## Gross Saving £840,000: "No Rubber-stamping"

### BRIGHTLINGSEA LINE IS INCLUDED

Mr. Ernest Marples, Transport Minister, announced yesterday that he had consented to 21 more railway closures, representing a gross saving of £840,000 a year, but he denied that he was "rubber-stamping" Dr. Beeching's Railway Board proposals.

"Closures are not a foregone conclusion," he told a Press conference in London—and exemplified that by refusing to consent to two proposed closures, one in Wales and the other in Scotland.

**The Minister is supporting Dr. Beeching's proposals to make the railways pay by approving eleven closures in England, eight in Scotland and two in the borders, as well as the shutting of the branch of the Central Wales line between Ontardulais and Swansea.**

Among the closures are the Brightlingsea-Wivenhoe line, subject to additional bus services and re-routing of some existing services; Thetford-Swaffham, subject to new bus services for workpeople and schoolchildren; and Dereham-Wells-next-the-Sea (Norfolk), subject to extra bus services.

"The pattern of these decisions is, I think, significant," said Mr. Marples. "Some people think I have just a yes-no decision to make, but most of my consents are 'yes, but . . .'"

Some were consents with no conditions except maintenance of existing bus services; others were consents with special requirements for extra bus services; others were consents deferred to give time for road improvements; and yet others were consents with the proviso that warning must be given if the railways board wished to take up the track.

In about half of the cases announced yesterday bus services were to be subsidised, and the average subsidy was about five per cent. of the saving from closing of the line. These subsidies would cost £40,000 a year out of the gross saving.

Last year, he recalled, the annual operating loss had been reduced by about £17 million, but unremunerative passenger services which the Board wanted to close were costing the taxpayer at least £30 million a year in subsidy.

# *The Last Train Gets A Grand Farewell*

### NEARLY 'LOCKED IN' AT ALDEBURGH

**PACKED with train enthusiasts, ordinary passengers and dozens of non-train users who just went along for the ride, the last passenger train made the trip along the eight-mile-long Saxmundham to Aldeburgh branch on Saturday evening.**

Minister of Transport, Mrs. Barbara Castle, gave her consent to the closure of the 106-year-old branch line in July, subject to the provision of additional bus services. The decision was made at the same time as the Minister refused to permit the proposed withdrawal of passenger services from the East Suffolk line.

In future there will be a total of 12 connections of buses with trains at Saxmundham to Lowestoft or Ipswich. The timetable for the new service, number 410, was published recently and comes into operation today.

In the morning the first bus/train connection will be made at Saxmundham for Ipswich at 7.26. For this, a bus leaves Aldeburgh at 6.50. The last in the evenings is at 6.50, the bus arriving at Aldeburgh at 7.27. The buses will take their usual route, going through Leiston, Aldringham and Thorpeness.

Season tickets and 12 weekly tickets will be issued on this service at standard rates, subject, according to the timetable, "to certain conditions."

A single fare on the bus from Saxmundham to Aldeburgh will cost 2s.3d., return 4s.

#### Crossing Gates Padlocked

The last train left Saxmundham just before 7 o'clock, already crowded with people. It picked up more passengers at Leiston and Thorpeness, before being greeted by a platform packed with several hundred people at Aldeburgh.

Among this crowd, which included officials and members of Aldeburgh Borough Council and East Suffolk Travellers' Association, was a small boy, dressed in the top hat and tails of an undertaker.

With fog detonators exploding under its wheels, the train left Aldeburgh a little behind time.

Two miles, and a few minutes later on, it stopped for the last time at Thorpeness Halt, its platform buildings decorated with bunting, borrowed for the occasion from Aldeburgh Borough Council.

And there it was forced to stay for some minutes. It was discovered that after the train had gone through to Aldeburgh, the crossing gates, reopened to road traffic, had been chained and padlocked by a group of people, believed to be holidaymakers from Thorpeness.

#### Ticket Souvenirs

But with the help of crowbars, railwaymen soon released the gates, and, to the roar of more fog "shots," the train rolled on. Following more detonations on the rails at Leiston, the twin diesel unit crossed the points on to the Ipswich/Lowestoft main line for the last time, 15 minutes late.

At Saxmundham station the driver, Mr. A. E. Skeels, of Ipswich, over 50 years a railwayman, was cornered by autograph hunters in the melee on the platform.

Ticket stocks were near-exhausted at Leiston, Aldeburgh and Saxmundham as hundreds of people clamoured for their souvenirs. At Leiston, it was estimated that between 350 and 400, including platform tickets, were sold. According to the booking clerk, thousands more had been sent away to collectors and other interested people.

However, it was not the last train to use the branch line, for a freight service will be maintained as far as Leiston's siding.

# Explosion and Anti-Beeching Shouts as Last Train Leaves

THERE was an explosion of warning detonators and shouts of "Down with Beeching" from young season-ticket holders in fancy-dress and black top-hats, when the last passenger train left Maldon East station for Witham last night.

Among passengers making the return trip on the 12-minutes-each-way run (1s. 6d. cheap day return) were Maldon's Mayor and Mayoress, Mr. and Mrs. W. S. Hutchinson.

Said Mr. Hutchinson: "This is a sad day. The closure of the passenger service is a retrograde step. It is untimely and unnecessary and takes place just at a time when the number of passengers was increasing.

People were beginning to realise the advantages of living in Maldon and commuting to London—a 61-minute run."

Mr. Hutchinson said that the local committee, which had fought hard for the line's retention, felt they had been let down by the M.P. for Maldon, Mr. Brian Harrison, who had put it on record that he believed in the Beeching report, and Maldon R.D.C., who had everything to gain and nothing to lose by giving their support to the campaign.

#### MOURNING VEIL

Two hundred people gathered at Maldon for the final send-off, and most boarded the train. They included a woman wearing a mourning veil and regular commuters to London carrying a placard reading "Down with Beeching, not with Maldon."

Railway preservationists travelled from London to make the final journey and obtain tickets for their collection.

# . . . More Bangs at Haverhill

TWO railwaymen were the only people on the platform at Haverhill station last night to see the last passenger train run on the branch line between Bartlow and Audley End.

The 56-seater diesel rail bus was crowded with passengers, who were mainly rail enthusiasts. Some travelled from London to make the journey.

There were several loud explosions from detonators, which had been put on the lines, and an extra toot from the driver as the train left Haverhill.

One of the passengers was Mr. Mick Cornish, prospective Labour candidate for Saffron Walden and secretary of the Preservation Society for the Stour Valley line. He said the loss of this traffic will strengthen the railway's case for closing the Stour Valley line.

# £100,000 BID FOR PART OF STOUR LINE

BUSINESSMAN and "steam" enthusiast, Mr. R. A. Lane, managing director of the Elm Bridge Plate Co., of Dovers Lane, Raynham, has bid £100,000 for the major part of the "axed" Sudbury-Shelford railway line—but British Rail wants £450,000.

Yesterday Mr. Lane said he would raise the cash on behalf of the Stour Valley Railway Preservation Society. "I think the track should be maintained," he said. "It would be a tourist attraction and I am sure could operate on a business footing."

Of B.R.'s £450,000 valuation for the whole stretch of line—which they say has been the price tag since October—he observed, "It's a ridiculous figure. We've asked for a site plan and not got one yet. Rightly or wrongly it could look as if they want to get the track torn up before negotiations start.

"If they do that and sell the stations separately, the bed of the track just becomes a liability."

#### 30 MILES OF TRACK

Over 30 miles of track are involved and a British Rail spokesman said yesterday that it made no difference to them whether these were torn up for scrap or used to transport tourists. "The price is still £450,000."

To which Mr. Lane responds that the railways have not even sought building permission on the sites they value so highly.

He will not stipulate exactly what length of the line he is interested in, other than to say it is "substantial".

The Stour Valley Preservation Society first revealed plans for a scheme to run steam trains on part of the closed line last August. Then the stretch between Sudbury and Haverhill was being considered, with one of the stations on the line being used as the society's headquarters.

The secretary, Mr. Wallace Banks of Hornchurch, has had discussions with Mr. Lane over the proposed purchase.

A price of £3,000 to £5,000 per mile of track was originally indicated by B.R., but it is not clear whether this includes the stations and their site areas.

# *Closure objectors will be at station as Minister arrives*

A DEMONSTRATION against the proposed closure of the Stour Valley railway line will be staged outside Sudbury station on Friday night when Mr. Peter Shore, Secretary of State for Economic Affairs, arrives to speak at a dinner in the town.

A large number of the demonstrators will be residents from Great Cornard Greater London Council overspill estate, who say they will be cut off from their friends and relatives outside the area if the line closes.

Leading them will be Mrs. Sylvia Byham, a local representative on Melford Rural Council, who said yesterday that the Londoners were "very upset" about the proposed closure.

"It is a hard enough job getting Londoners to settle here with the present facilities and if they are cut off from London they will be going back left, right and centre. Many are thoroughly disillusioned and feel they have been brought to the area under false pretences," said Mrs. Byham.

She added that the demonstration would be a peaceful one and she was trying to organise local folk singers to make a musical protest.

Mr. Shore will be speaking at the annual dinner of the West Suffolk Fabian Society.

#### 1,160 written objections

Written objections to the proposed closure of the line have now leaped to 1,160 with Friday being the last day for objections to be sent to the Transport Users' Consultative Committee.

"This is a very good figure and beyond my committee's best expectations," said Mr. Alan Phillips, legal adviser to the Sudbury and District Railway Action Committee.

"The number of objections is indicative of the volume of local public opinion which is in strong opposition to the proposed closure," he said.

On Monday, Sudbury and Woodbridge M.P., Mr. Keith Stainton, will be meeting the action committee and local authority representatives at Sudbury to discuss the proposed closure.

Newspaper articles from the 1960s.
*Courtesy East Anglian Daily Times*

method for calculating the losses was distorted to increase perceived costs for individual lines. It did not take into account economies that could be made, or aspects such as running fewer trains with higher fares. The consequences of closing feeder lines on the remaining network was not properly considered, including the additional costs that the remaining lines would need to contribute to the central administration. The outcome was that railways continued to lose even more money once secondary routes and branches were pruned and their traffic contribution to the wider network was lost.

The survey was flawed. For example, the receipts at holiday destinations were used, as opposed to their overall use by passengers who mostly purchased their tickets elsewhere; whilst the timing of the single survey, in a slack period, provided a false portrayal of lower use. The resulting list for the closure of lines was therefore equally flawed. The principle of closing duplicated routes was taken to absurd extremes. I could go on, but in his defence a number of secondary lines had outlived their usefulness and needed closing; at the time the car was really coming into its own, some trains were running almost empty and it was a concise report with good maps.

> **Weekdays and Sundays.**
>
> **The service between Havant and Hayling Island is withdrawn.**
>
> Passenger road services are operated in the area by Southdown Motor Services Ltd.

Timetable closure information 1964.

| Table 74→ | WALSALL AND DUDLEY |
| --- | --- |
| | The service on this table is withdrawn and Wednesbury Town, Great Bridge North, Dudley Port Low Level and Dudley stations are closed. The locality is served by Omnibuses operated by Walsall Corporation Transport, the Birmingham and Midland Motor Omnibus Co. Ltd., West Bromwich Corporation Transport and Birmingham City Transport. |
| Table 75→ | STAFFORD, WELLINGTON AND SHREWSBURY |
| | The local passenger service on this table is withdrawn and Gnosall, Newport, Donnington, Trench Crossing, Hadley, Admaston Halt, Walcot and Upton Magna stations are closed. The locality is served by buses operated by G. H. Austin and Sons Ltd., Shropshire Omnibus Association Ltd., Williamsons Motorways and the Birmingham and Midland Omnibus Co. Ltd.<br><br>For train service between Wellington and Shrewsbury, see Table 65. |

It should also be noted that the Beeching Report only contained recommendations. Final decisions on closures were taken by government ministers after consideration by a Transport Users' Consultative Committee. The law was changed to ensure these committee hearings had very narrow terms of reference and non-binding recommendations. If any alternative bus service was available, they effectively became rubber stamps to the closure process.

The biggest blunders involved the closures related to the notion of an apparent duplication of lines to key locations, even where these lines were well used. This led to busy main lines serving entirely different areas between major centres being singled out for services to be withdrawn. This ill-judged butchery resulted in the closure of the Waverley Route, since partially reopened and a great success. The Great Central north of Aylesbury was closed on the same basis. It is arguable that had it remained, with its continental loading gauge, it would have usefully provided extra capacity, particularly for freight and possibly it may even have resulted in different outcomes for the design and cost of HS2.

Elsewhere in the country, important and busy lines such as York–Hull via Market Weighton, Peterborough–Grimsby via Louth, Harrogate–Northallerton via Ripon and Bournemouth–Bath via Radstock and Blandford were all recommended to have services withdrawn, as the end points could all eventually be reached by other longer routes. They were all closed, although the Liverpool–Southport and Richmond–Broad Street lines were reprieved from closure. The reprieved lines thrive, as the others most probably would have done.

Other blunders can be found throughout the country. In East Anglia, Haverhill was designated as an expanding town at the same time as its railway was recommended for closure. It is said the Polegate–Eridge route, known as the Cuckoo Line, together with some others in the south were closed because, politically, all the closures could not be in the north. Numerous important feeder lines, where no real attempt was made to rationalise and encourage traffic, were closed. This included recommendations to close lines that were indicated as being busy to coastal resorts such as Hornsea, Withernsea, Gorleston, Ventnor, Porthcawl, Whitby and Minehead, but where, once again, fares would have mostly been generated elsewhere on the network

In Scotland and Wales, a number of closures are today considered to have been big and expensive mistakes. In London, an example of a line proposed for closure by Beeching was Clapham Junction–Kensington Olympia; the latter station is now used by over five million passengers a year.

Some of the worst blunders were perpetuated after Beeching's removal; by continuing in his quest for profitability more and busier feeder routes were cut. Beeching never recommended the closure of the Oxford–Cambridge, Derby–Manchester, Stratford-upon-Avon–Cheltenham, Cowdenbeath–Perth and Woodhead main lines. He also never included lines for closure such as to Alnwick, Blackpool Central, Dereham, Fawley, Fleetwood, Hunstanton, Kingswear, Leven, St Andrews, Swanage and Wisbech. These further closures, offset by lines recommended for closure in the Beeching Report that were reprieved, together with later closures and reopened lines, resulted in the surviving national network we have today.

Finally, Dr Beeching only made recommendations; the real blame lies with both Conservative and Labour Government Transport Ministers, in particular Ernest Marples, but also Tom Fraser and Barbara Castle who actually implemented the majority of closures. For all his faults, many people have heard of Dr Beeching, he did plan a modern future for the railways, some cuts were inevitable and, of course, hindsight is a wonderful thing!

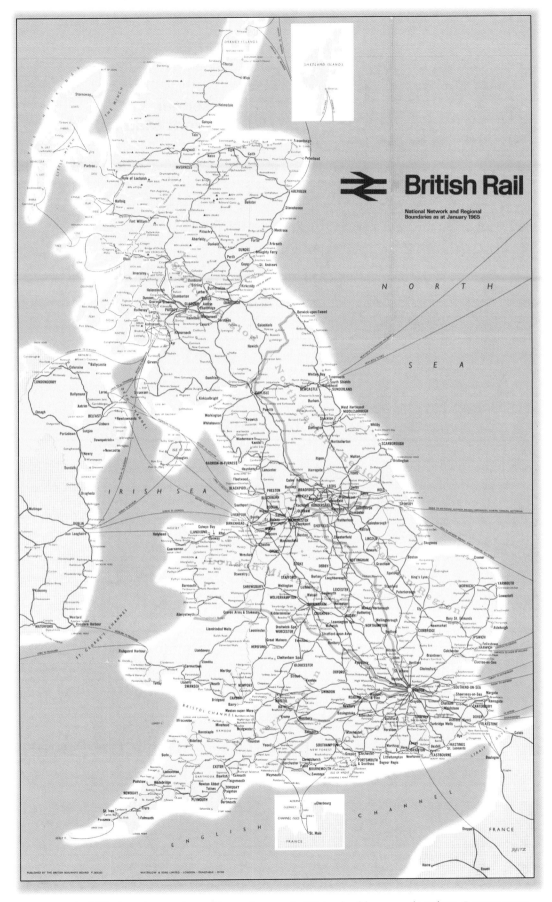

BR map of 1965, showing regions. Many closures in Wales had been undertaken. Routes once shown as main lines, such as the ex-S&D and the ex-LSWR routes west of Exeter, had been reduced to secondary status, except oddly between Wadebridge and Padstow.

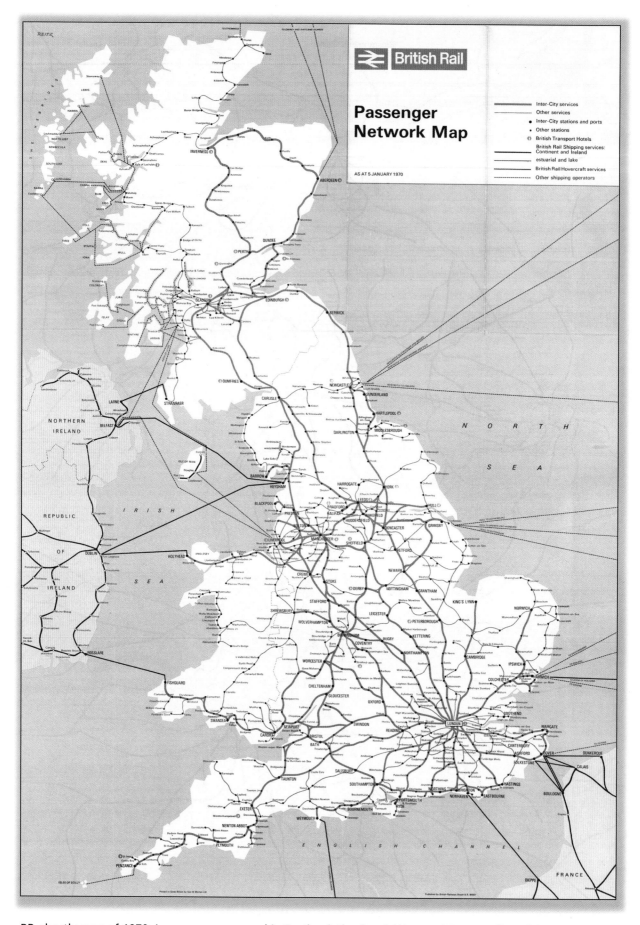

BR ghostly map of 1970. Large gaps appeared in Scotland, the South West and East Anglia. All lines in the Lincolnshire coast area had been reduced in status, prior to extensive closures.

# 13
# Behind closed doors

The closure of many railways by BR in the 1960s was shrouded in an unreasonable lack of transparency. This can perhaps be traced back to the earlier days of private railways when commercial decisions could be made, including those to close lines, behind closed doors and with minimal formal procedures. Whilst this could result in indignant local and even parliamentary protests, together with the occasional legal challenge, some closures were implemented with short notice.

The strategic importance of railways in two world wars also spawned a need for transport secrecy. During World War 1, many rail-served armaments factories, together with military and navel depots, were established. One such depot was near Barnham station on the Bury–Thetford line. The small depot in deepest rural East Anglia included a big secret in that it was used for the storage of mustard gas to combat Germany's poison gases.

At Woolwich the existing railways within the Royal Arsenal were brought together under the Royal Arsenal Railways in 1891. Eventually narrow, mixed and standard-gauge lines extended to almost 150 miles, creating the most complex and densest railway network in Britain. Hidden behind high walls and doors the armaments site was sometimes known as the 'Secret City'. The railways reached a peak of activity during World War 1 when over 60 locomotives could be in daily use. The arsenal and its remaining railways closed in 1967.

In Scotland, near Gretna, a huge munitions factory was established during World War 1. With about 125 miles of narrow-gauge line and 34 locomotives, the factory produced over 800 tonnes of ammunition a week. The remote location was chosen as it was hoped mists

The Midland Railway Offices' imposing door at Liverpool, seen in October 2006. A Chairman of the Mid-Suffolk Light Railway once speculated in MR shares. This lead to concern that the MR were looking to use an upgraded MSLR to expand their empire to a new East Coast port, in an attempt to challenge the GER's monopoly at Harwich. *Author*

One of two blocked-up utilitarian entrances that led from Regent Road to Huskisson Dock station on the closed Liverpool Overhead Railway, noted in October 2006. The railway was making a profit and paying shareholders, but deferring expensive maintenance on the metal overhead structure. They miscalculated that such an important line would be financially bailed out by others. *Author*

and natural tree cover would obscure the site. Although mostly abandoned after the war a munitions factory on part of the site at Eastriggs had its remaining 20 miles of narrow-gauge track offered for sale in 2016.

During World War 2 many military depots were also served by the railways. For example, the Royal Ordnance Factory at Bishopton, in Scotland, opened in 1941 and was provided with 80 miles of narrow-gauge line. On a smaller scale underground stone mines also made ideal bomb-proof ammunition stores. Taking just Wiltshire as an example, at Corsham near Box Hill Tunnel an underground military depot was established. It was even said that the strategic reserve of steam engines, a secret reserve of coal-fired locomotives to be used in the event of an oil crisis, was kept here. Sadly, it was so secret no one has ever been able to find it! Elsewhere in the county Monkton Farleigh was a rail-served underground munitions depot, whilst narrow-gauge lines went underground to serve an ammunition bunker for RAF Chilmark and remained intact until 1995.

In Wales, priceless artworks were stored in a slate mine at Manod during World War 2, the trip from Bangor being by LMS road vehicles, with drivers sworn to secrecy. In the Rhydymwyn Valley, near Flint, a line ran to a factory that at one time produced mustard gas shells during World War 2, before moving on to create enriched uranium for the first atomic bombs.

World War 2 spawned other confidences. New lines were built to provide flexibility in the event of bomb damage. The line to Cairnryan was shrouded in secrecy. It branched off the Stranraer line near Castle Kennedy and was built to substitute in the event of Glasgow's port facilities being damaged. Secret experiments with concrete Mulberry Harbours for the D-Day landings were undertaken at the port here. Elsewhere and out of the public gaze, the Royal Navy Dockyard railways at Chatham and Portsmouth were very busy, but by the early 1980s were out of use.

The railways were run from less-obvious headquarters during World War 2, such as the SR from Dorking and the LMS from Watford. All the Big Four moved some offices

The Florentine-styled door allowed coal into the Wallasey Central Hydraulic Tower at Birkenhead Docks and is viewed here in September 2006. The docks at Birkenhead were considered a threat to those at Liverpool and at one time Liverpool Corporation used public money to buy land at Birkenhead in an effort to thwart growth. There was much disquiet when this was discovered and the land was sold. *Author*

*Right:* A Dutch Renaissance door at Nottingham Victoria seen in January 2008. Opening on Queen Victoria's birthday in 1900, it was called Victoria rather than Central station. Closed in September 1967, a possible rail route through the new proposals was not retained, but the Lower Parliament Street railway bridge is still buried within the new development. *Author*

*Below:* A tiny door with a big secret, seen in September 1997. Below the distinctive façade of London Down Street station, closed in May 1932, were secret bomb proof war offices. These were used in World War 2 by Winston Churchill before the Cabinet War Rooms were completed. The Railway Executive Committee also operated from the offices that had been created deep below ground. *Author*

out from the cities. Down Street underground station, which was closed to regular passengers in 1932, was converted for use by the Railway Executive Committee during the war and was also secretly used for a time by the War Cabinet. It is said War Ministers rode in the cabs of underground trains to attend meetings here.

The LBSCR provided an elegant, almost country house porch, entrance to some of its rural stations. Mayfield was one of the stations on the Cuckoo Line and is seen in April 1995. The line was effectively sabotaged by BR in that a new timetable was introduced on the busy route that deliberately made services and connections inconvenient. Closure was therefore able to be put into effect. *Author*

The SR entrance, dating from 1927 and seen in May 1995, to South Western House in Southampton. Formally a hotel, it is suggested the original staircase was used as a basis for the design of that on the *Titanic*. Guests also stayed here before boarding the *Titanic* and it is even said you can occasionally hear echoes of those who perished in the icy waters. *Author*

The York headquarters offices of the NER opened in 1906 and the imposing entrance, in a Baroque Revival style, is seen in October 2016. In a twist of fate, the railway offices were sold in 2005 and are now a hotel, whilst the original railway hotel, located opposite, was converted into offices after the current Royal Station Hotel opened in 1878. *Author*

Pocklington station opened in 1847 on the York–Hull line. On threat of closure it was shown the line could make a profit, but a loss of £100,000 was conjured up by BR. A protester from Pocklington pointed out that this was a typing error, yet the line closed in November 1965. Go through the door here in September 1995 and you would have found a sports hall under the high-hipped overall roof. *Author*

Hornsea Town station fell into a state of disrepair after closure in October 1964 and was almost demolished, until the buildings were listed in 1979. It still remains and the entrance is seen in June 1966. A secret bunker, at nearby Rise, housed troops trained in guerrilla warfare during World War 2 in case of a coastal invasion of this area by Germany. *Author*

London Bishopsgate. If you could get through this entrance, pictured in September 1997, a volleyball pitch would have been found on the other side. When it was a goods station fish traffic was also handled, whilst wagons of spirits would also be unloaded in a bonded store to prevent customs delays. Fire destroyed the main building and killed two customs officers in 1964. *Author*

Railway tunnels were also used in World War 2. The Aldwych tunnels were closed for the duration and stored priceless exhibits from the British Museum. Swainsley Tunnel on the closed Leek & Manifold Railway was used to store munitions. The closed Clifton Rocks Railway was used to send radio broadcasts for the BBC. Maenclochog Tunnel in Wales was used for bomb target practice. The Tunnel Railway at Ramsgate was used as an air-raid shelter as were many other tunnels, particularly in London.

Some stations and halts that were 'unadvertised' in public timetables were intended only for those who needed to know. Examples range from Priory Halt for Admiralty staff only, to Cranwell for RAF personnel and the army base station at Bovington Camp. No less than seven halts were provided on Devonport's dock lines for military personnel and almost a dozen were provided for training on the Longmoor Military Railway.

After the war the culture of privacy continued. Although BR offices were accessible to the public, the public were not really welcome; the BR headquarters at Marylebone was not called 'the Kremlin' for nothing. That was in part because at the time there was no public right to information and the operation of the railways often continued to be shrouded in secrecy. If BR wanted to close a line, they could provide whatever figures they wanted to prove the case. Behind closed doors they could deliberately destroy lines, by making the timetable increasingly unusable and inflating costs.

Objectors to BR's proposals to close railway services were not allowed to question any of the information in the written brief, nor was any discussion about the way in which a service had been, or might have been operated, allowed. Protestors were ruled out of order if they suggested BR had piled on the cost of a line, or had made no effort to trim costs.

There was often a complete lack of transparency behind receipts and costs for lines proposed for closure. Railwaymen were angry at the cold-blooded and deliberate murder of the ex-S&D line by the Western Region. There was outrage at the Eastern Region, who put an embargo on statistics for the Cambridge–Colchester route after one set of figures showed the line making a profit. They simply produced new figures showing it made a loss and when it was argued that this loss was small, they produced yet another set of figures showing an even bigger loss.

Closure procedures have since been made more stringent and transparent. This has led to some irregular and infrequent 'ghost trains', almost entirely unknown to the general public, running on a number of lines as an alternative to going through a long, formal and expensive closure process. Unlike earlier closures these lines and stations can easily spring back to life, but even today a few stations included in public timetables are just not accessible and can only be glimpsed behind closed doors.

# 14
# Last days of the branch line

Only a relatively few branch lines have survived, many remaining lines succumbing to the Beeching Report, except where bus substitution proved particularly difficult. The 'Lost Lines' series of books covers over 300 such branch lines, such as Cirencester, Framlingham and Richmond to name but a few. These branches were almost always intended as secondary feeder lines and survived because they were seen as part of a bigger picture. When looking at their histories, although individual, they are also quite similar, with themes relating to raising finance, steady growth until the 1920s, followed by a slow decline that accelerated rapidly after World War 2. The Buntingford branch in Hertfordshire typifies many of the issues that were encountered by British branch lines.

Buntingford was a market town that had fallen between the GER and GNR main lines. As a consequence, a branch line was proposed to serve the town and the Ware, Hadham & Buntingford Railway was born. However, there were objections from local landowners and the original route had to be altered, with the line eventually starting at St Margaret's, (spelt 's in timetables until closure). Buntingford was also built as a through station as it was initially planned that the branch would extend northward to join the Cambridge line near Shelford, enabling the line to also be used as a diversionary route. Again, after objections from landowners, this plan was thrown out by Parliament.

As in many cases, capital proved difficult to raise and the branch line had to be financially assisted by the Eastern Counties Railway, that in 1862 became the GER and operated the line from its opening. In spite of the problems and some shoddy construction that had to be rectified, the 13¾-mile St Margaret's–Buntingford branch opened in July 1863. The steepest gradient was 1 in 56, whilst the line crossed the River Rib and other watercourses several times. As with so many independent small railway companies, it soon merged with a larger pre-Grouping railway. In this case it became part of the GER in 1868.

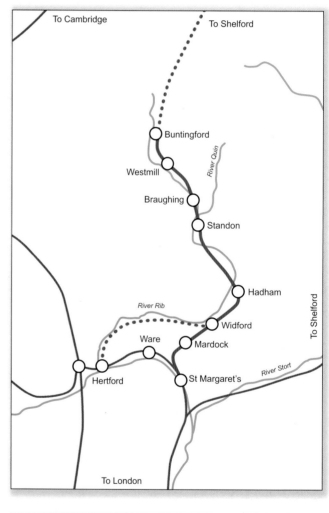

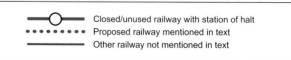

| | Closed/unused railway with station of halt |
| ....... | Proposed railway mentioned in text |
| | Other railway not mentioned in text |

Buntingford station in Hertfordshire in April 1964, with a DMU ready to depart for St Margaret's. My diary reports that dust blew up at the back of the DMU, which reached speeds of 75mph. The goods shed is to be noted, but there was ever-reducing freight at this time. The main station building is seen to the right and still survives. *Author*

Sometime after opening the branch became affectionately known as 'The Bunt' and the line and its staff became an important part of the rural life of the area. There was a gradual rise in both passenger and agricultural freight use. Some facilities were improved by the GER, some bridges strengthened, whilst the legal requirement for block working saw this installed on the branch by 1891 and represented the biggest expense since opening.

When the LNER took over they replaced some signals and track, together with undertaking repairs and painting of stations. They aimed to reduce costs at Braughing and Hadham by removing footbridges, down side platform canopies and toilets, together with closing the signal boxes on Sundays. They introduced some push-pull working on the line, before World War 2 curtailed further plans.

After World War 2 passenger traffic declined. In 1948 BR took over, affixing a huge dark blue enamel sign on Buntingford station buildings. Apart from new station signs, little was done to modernise the line or to attract traffic. Sunday services were withdrawn in 1955 and six signalling staff were made redundant in 1960, as trains became mainly peak hour only.

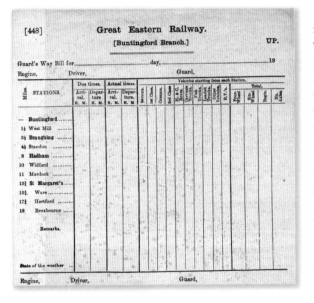

The GER Guard's Way Bill, showing mixed trains used the branch and that considerable paperwork was required.

Three-car DMUs replaced steam in 1959, as was the case with many branch lines. However, the introduction of DMUs saw the discontinuance of through peak-hour coaches onto the adjoining newly electrified lines to London. As car ownership increased, people gradually used other stations with direct electric services to London. As a consequence, patronage of the branch line actually fell as a result of DMU modernisation.

The branch was listed, together with most other remaining rural branch lines in Britain, for closure in the Beeching Report. Losses were inflated, with BR using false statistics for the branch, including the cost of the six signalling staff that no longer worked on the line, nine length men when only two were employed part time and the full cost of other staff that worked on the line for just a small part of their day. There were objections and protests, nevertheless closure was pushed through.

After just over a century of faithful service the line closed to passengers in November 1964 and to freight, which was mainly coal and agricultural produce, in September of the following year. The track was ripped up soon after final closure and unwanted structures on the line were demolished or just left to rot, although station buildings remain at Braughing and Buntingford.

*Above:* Standon had a single platform and a wooden building dating from 1869, after the original station was burnt down. The nearby Standon flower mill at one time had its own siding. The mill also had a hydro-electric plant using the River Rib and the station platforms were electrically lit from this in 1911. The station is seen in April 1964. *Author*

Braughing station with a view from the train in April 1964 of an attractive GER lower-quadrant signal beside the station master's house which dates from 1892. At this time the station was served on Mondays to Fridays by a peak-hour service only, with no trains between 09.36 and 15.53. Today an infrequent bus service runs only on certain days of the week. *Author*

*Above:* Hadham station with a waiting shelter, built to the same design as that at Braughing, viewed in April 1964. The shelters were once enclosed, with a fire place and toilet, together with a platform canopy, but these were removed to reduce costs by the LNER. Passenger services on the line ceased in November 1964. *Author*

Widford station in April 1964. The facilities included a waiting room, toilets and platform staff. Indeed, on some early BR maps the line was shown as a main route. The original waiting room is the middle building, which was retained after the far building was added by the GER in 1892. *Author*

After closure Braughing station descended into a perilous state of dilapidation. This view of the platform at Braughing, showing the brick-built waiting shelter and signal box in the distance, was taken in February 1983 almost two decades after closure. Fortunately, the buildings were later restored and even a new signal box was constructed. *Author*

Braughing signal box contained a 24-lever Saxby & Farmer frame. It once controlled the second largest goods yard on the Buntingford branch, which had a capacity of 50 wagons. In 1927 the LNER closed the box on Sundays, but it remained in use until closure of the line to passengers. Shortly after final closure to freight the block instruments were removed. It is seen in February 1983. *Author*

The dilapidated GER wooden shed on the platform at Braughing station in February 1983. Although employees were reduced on the branch, platform staff were maintained on the line and assisted travellers, together with general railway duties until passenger closure. *Author*

Buntingford station's steep gables viewed in July 2016. The brick building dates from 1863 and was the most substantial passenger structure on the branch. Built as a through station, the line was never extended northward. Buntingford station is now two homes and the former station yard area has been redeveloped. *Author*

The same wooden shed at Braughing in July 2016, over half a century after it was last used. The platform cabins were a feature of a number of stations on the branch. Apart from introducing DMUs, little attempt was made by BR to introduce real economies on the branch. *Author*

The restored waiting shelter at Braughing, with the concrete posts for the station's once dark blue enamel nameplate, seen in July 2016. Braughing and Hadham both at one time had covered footbridges connecting the platforms at these two passing loops on the single-line. Braughing station platforms were oil lit until closure. *Author*

Braughing station has been faithfully restored by the family of the former station master from a sorry state into a lovely residence. A static BR Mark 2 coach is seen at the station platform in July 2016, but reopening of the branch is unlikely. *Author*

A standard GER cast iron seat back from Standon, seen in July 2016. Quite a few relics of the line still exist and some have been preserved by the Buntingford Railway & Local History Society, who remain active in the area and whose aims include keeping alive memories of the line. *Author*

The cast iron side of a platform bench from Standon station displaying a fishing net, shellfish and fish, seen in July 2016. The unusual railway seat was originally intended for a coastal resort, but certainly this one managed to end up in Standon rather than Yarmouth or perhaps even Hunstanton. *Author*

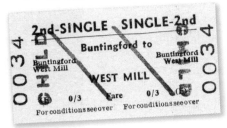

Subsequently some parts of the route have been returned to agriculture, whilst other sections of the trackbed are used as footpaths. Sadly, a similar story can be told about many other British branch lines. However, the Buntingford Railway & Local History Society have preserved relics of the branch and promote interest in the lost line.

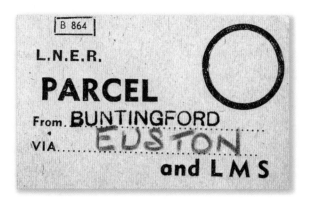

Looking initially a bit like a tree, a wooden signal post complete with some fittings still remains outside Hadham. It was originally No 26 signal which was the 'up' home. In view of its longevity it is possible that the original signal post was replaced in 1929. The 22ft (7m) wooden post is viewed in July 2016, over half a century after closure of the branch. *S. Ruff*

# 15
# Signals of change

Early trains were relatively slow and sometimes infrequent, but as the network and its use grew, some sort of system to direct trains and keep them clear of each other was required. Forms of hand signalling were used early on to try and prevent accidents. Many different types of early signals developed, plain red disks being popular, but the semaphore signal that can still be recognised today was generally introduced in the 1840s. Lower-quadrant signals became widely used, but an accident on the ECML where snow and ice prevented the arm from being raised to the danger position led to more use of upper-quadrant signals.

A number of accidents culminating in that on the now closed Armagh–Warrenpoint line in 1889 in Northern Ireland, which killed over 80 people, led within a very short space of time to the legal requirement for block working. It was recognised that trains cannot collide with each other if only one train at a time occupies a section of track. In basic terms, railway lines were divided into sections known as 'blocks' which are fixed, mostly between two signal boxes. Before a train enters a block, the signalman must make sure it is not occupied by another train. At the same time the interlocking of points and signalling, that meant signal box levers could only be moved if it was safe to do so, also became a legal requirement.

On single-lines, a physical token of some kind was ferried back and forth over a section. Single-line sections, such as on the M&GN and S&D, used Whitaker's automatic tablet-exchanging equipment which was so successful in speeding trains that the doubling of all track was never completed. The sound in the signal box of the tinkle of semaphore codes announcing train movements accompanied all such equipment.

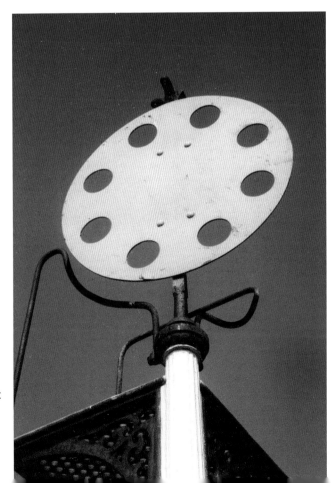

Early signals, such as this used on the Ffestiniog Railway, displayed a prominent red disc when facing the train to indicate stop, or danger. This would have been turned through 180 degrees to denote clear, or proceed. A lamp would have been mounted on top of the disk. They fell out of use in the 1920s as traffic on the line declined. *Author*

An example of a MR crossbar-style signal that operated on the Burton-on-Trent brewery system, seen in September 1993. At its peak 1,000 wagons a day could be handled on the network of private lines. There were also 30 level crossings and traffic congestion could occur. By 1967 the network was mostly out of use. *Author*

Numerous different designs of signal boxes and equipment also developed, although the underlying safety principles were similar. Many signal boxes were built of wood because the top part at least had to have windows and good visibility to see the trains. The lever frames and signalling equipment was mostly supplied by private firms; examples include Saxby & Farmer, Ransome & Rapier and McKenzie & Holland.

There were several types of signal posts, made from metal, wood and concrete. Some are instantly recognisable, including those of the Big Four. The GWR centre pivot on a tubular steel post with a GWR finial is probably the best known. Unlike most others their signals remained resolutely lower quadrant. Some SR signals were made from old sections of rail. The LNER and LMS signals were to be found on a range of posts, but all with upper-quadrant arms and finials replaced by practical post caps.

To achieve maximum visibility the heights of signal posts varied, but signal arms were relatively constant, with yellow for caution and red for stop being widely used by the 1920s. Many signals were located in remote areas and most were lit by paraffin or rape oil. Where available, electricity and even gas was sometimes used to illuminate the signal spectacle glasses. As to the spectacle glasses themselves, interestingly, the green lights were often produced by a blue glass, which when illuminated by a yellow flame resulted in a green light.

A disused line to Portsmouth Naval Base, still with a double-drop arm signal, in the early 1980s. The secretive system was obscured behind high walls and gates with spiked tops. The once extensive network was busy until closed by the Navy in 1978. Today some isolated sections of track can still be found. *Author*

Signal on a disused freight line at St Helens, seen in September 2006. The tall metal post was to assist with visibility. Signalling equipment has sometimes been retained on 'mothballed' railway lines in case any future use is required. Many wooden posts were replaced by more durable tubular metal posts. *Author*

During the early days of BR, a bewildering array of different signals still existed, many going back to the pre-Grouping companies. The somersault signals of the GNR, M&GN and a few other railways were most unusual in that they were designed to be up to vertical when 'off' (clear). Signalling for many decades was typified by rationalisation, as the level of traffic fell on parts of the railways. On branches and lesser used lines, costs were sometimes reduced by some signals being left in the 'off' position, such as on Sundays, as signalmen's shifts were reduced, whilst block lengths were also on occasion increased with intermediate signal boxes being closed. On a number of secondary and branch lines, more modern signalling methods were introduced, but in many instances few real economies were implemented, thereby enhancing the financial case for closure.

In the wider context advances in signalling were made, such as the detection of trains through track circuits and automated signal boxes covering wide areas with automatic colour-light signalling. This trend is continuing with state-of-the-art digital signals, resulting in semaphore signals becoming ever rarer.

This has all resulted in the loss of the traditional signal box. A number of interesting manual signal boxes have been listed as being of historic importance, but many more have not and face an uncertain future as their size and location often makes reuse difficult. In 1948 it is estimated there were about 10,000 signal boxes in use, in 2015 there were 373 and this figure will reduce eventually to just a dozen or so key signalling centres.

After lines closed signal boxes were stripped of their equipment and many were just left to be vandalised or rot away. Signal posts could also remain in place, but usually stripped of their signal arms; in some cases they remained for years, particularly if they were not metal and had negligible scrap value. After the closure of the M&GN a number of signals were still illuminated by their paraffin lamps for up to four weeks, but the trains never returned.

The signal guarding the swing bridge to Hayling Island. The branch was running at a profit, but a sudden need to replace the bridge was put forward as the reason to close the line and this was implemented in November 1963. The SR signal post, made from old sections of railway line, is viewed at Langstone in Hampshire in June 1985, long after closure. *Author*

*Above:* An GNR somersault signal at Tumby Woodside in Lincolnshire seen in August 1964. These signals were unique in that they somersaulted from horizontal for danger to almost vertical for clear. The signal was used right up to closure of the station in October 1970. *Author*

*Above:* Ipswich Docks with a wooden post semaphore signal guarding trains coming up from the docks to the Top Yard. The signal post caps have been removed, but the signal, seen in September 2011, still existed in thicker undergrowth in 2017. This dock branch was formally closed in March 2012, although the last working was in 2006. *Author*

**BLEDLOW GROUND FRAME**

A derelict semaphore signal remaining near Silvertown, at London Docklands in September 1997. It is interesting that although the adjoining PLA system once extended to about 140 miles of line, several freight sections operated with flagmen rather than signals, before its closure in 1970. *Author*

A signal gantry at Tunbridge Wells West. The LBSCR post finials have been removed at the same time as the signal arms. At its peak the station was once served by over 130 trains a day. The station closed in July 1985 and the view was taken in July 1989, but the heritage Spa Valley Railway now uses part of the site. *Author*

*Above:* Llangwyllog station on the Amlwch branch had an open-air lever frame that was operated by a porter signalman. It is seen from the train in July 1964. The ex-LNWR line and station closed to passengers in December of the same year, although through freight survived on the route to the Octel works at Amlwch until 1993. *Author*

*Above right:* The narrow-gauge Vale of Rheidol distinctive lower-quadrant signal seen in August 1964. The narrow-gauge signal finial was not the same as the GWR standard-gauge designs. The signal guarded a level crossing on an original section of line at Aberystwyth, a short section which is now closed on this heritage railway. *Author*

*Right:* On some lightly used lines, traditional signalling was removed. Here a stop board was provided before the crossing gates and has the same status as a traditional stop signal. The signal board was noted in September 1994 at Histon on the Cambridge–St Ives branch which was used for sand trains until closure in May 1992. The line has since been turned into a guided busway. *Author*

The GN & GE Joint Committee distinctive signal box at Postland, on the March–Spalding main line, in August 2008. The final train to use this route was in November 1982, making this one of the very last major closures. The box, which retained its levers, was set for preservation in the USA, but never made it. *Author*

Bristol Old Station signal box provided a good overview of the station. When the original GWR station was extended in 1878 the design cleverly arched over the existing signal box. The box was taken out of use in September 1965, when residual traffic was transferred to Temple Meads station. It is viewed in September 1993 and still remains today. *Author*

A colour-light signal guarding Weymouth station from the harbour tramway. Although the tramway was last used in May 1999, the signal, viewed here, was still operational at the end of 2017. The line had been given a 'permanent out of use' status in 2016. *Author*

Annesley signal box in the Leen Valley is of typical MR design. The MR were unique in designing both their own signal boxes and signalling frame, as private signalling contractors were widely employed prior to 1923. The box was used as a shunter's cabin before demolition. It is seen in May 1985, after the sidings and signalling had been removed. *Author*

Some CR signal boxes had striking deeply-set windows and a heavily overhanging roof, likely to be helpful in snowy conditions. Such a styled signal box is pictured at St Fillans station in October 2011. The signal box and station buildings survive as listed buildings, although the line closed to passengers in October 1951. *Capt. J. Roddis*

*Right:* Hindolvestone signal box in Norfolk on the M&GN. The signalling bells rang silent in the small, but distinctively designed, well preserved signal box in February 1959. It is seen here in April 2009 some 50 years after closure and still survives. The station itself was once commended in the best station competition. *Author*

*Below:* Alresford signal box showing very little roof overhang. A categorisation system is used by the Signalling Record Society and as such this box is a LSWR Type 1, built to a standard design by the LSWR. The preserved operational signal box is seen on the Watercress Line in January 2017. *Author*

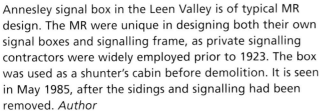

A modern signal box was built in 1950 by BR to a LNER design at Murrow West in Cambridgeshire, where the ex-GN & GE Joint Committee line crossed on the level with the ex-M&GN line. It was in use until April 1966 and is seen in August 2008. *Author*

A signal box at Washford on the heritage West Somerset Railway houses a replica of the interior of the S&D Midford signal box. It shows the complex array of telegraph block instruments and signalling equipment associated with working a railway. Created by the Somerset & Dorset Railway Trust Museum, it is viewed in June 2009. *Author's collection*

A GWR-styled signal box, originally from Cradley Heath, is pictured in July 2001, having been saved and re-sited at the Birmingham Railway Museum at Tyseley. The signal box was subsequently moved to the South Devon Railway at Totnes and is now called Ashburton Junction. *Author*

# Ten Great British lost main lines

The problem with selecting just 10 or so lost main lines is that there are, of course, more candidates. I have no doubt some will consider others are worthier, but this is my personal short list. Almost all were closed simply because they were judged to be duplicated by other routes; they were mostly well used, predominantly double-track and some were of considerable length. In many cases a concerted effort to close the lines was mounted by BR. Some main lines were reduced in status to that of a branch line on 1960s railway maps. Services were often slowed down and diverted onto alternative routes. The threat of closure dissuaded passengers and many stations took on an air of dereliction.

The ex-NBR Waverley route at Melrose, seen in March 1993, after the most contentious of closures in January 1969. Although eventually reduced in status on BR maps to a branch line, it was operated as a main line to the end. The northern part of the railway has since been reopened and Melrose station and its unusual platform canopy hopefully await the return of trains. *Author*

## The Waverley Route

The closure of the 98-mile ex-NBR double-track main Edinburgh–Carlisle line, to become famously known as the Waverley Route, was one of the most controversial of the Beeching proposals. The line opened in its entirety in 1849. It ran through important towns such as Hawick and Galashiels in the Borders of Scotland, which were once served by trains such as the 'Thames-Forth Express'. It was seen in the Beeching Report simply to duplicate the ex-CR Carlisle–Edinburgh route via Carstairs, although it served an entirely different area. A huge fight was mounted against closure, but all to no avail. In January 1969, the Waverley route was closed to passengers and BR quickly lifted the track at Riddings Junction to demonstrate their determination to kill the line for good.

But this was not to be the end. The Scottish Government took the bold step and reversed the closure. This saw the re-opening of the 35-mile northern Edinburgh–Tweedbank section in 2015. The use of this new line has been hugely successful with use well up on forecasts. It is hopefully only a matter of time before the entire route is reopened.

The ex-LNWR Oxford–Cambridge route seen at Potton in September 1994. The railway connected the university towns of Oxford and Cambridge, together with linking East Anglia with the west of England. The line was divided between three BR regions, all with different views as to its value and sections were closed between 1968 and May 1993. There are plans to reopen much of the western section. *Author*

# Oxford–Cambridge (The Varsity Line)

Perhaps not quite a main line in every sense, but the 76-mile ex-LNWR double-track line connecting the university cities of Oxford and Cambridge was once an important cross-country route. It linked no less than seven main lines and conveyed significant freight. Its closure was not even proposed by Beeching, but an inconsistent approach was taken by the government to closure proposals put forward by the three BR regions that covered the route. The Eastern and Western regions were given permission to close their sections, but the Bedford–Bletchley section, on the LMR, was reprieved from closure. The result was that the line ceased to be used as a through Oxford–Cambridge route in January 1968.

History repeated itself on proposals for reopening. Your author was once involved in regional planning guidance for the Milton Keynes & South Midlands area. The South East Region's part of the plan included reopening the 31-mile Oxford–Bletchley section.

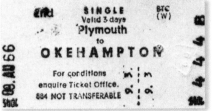
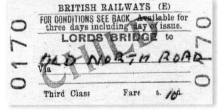

The Eastern Region took a different view and would not include any reopening policies for the Cambridge–Bedford section in their part of the same plan. Fortunately, proposals for restoring services between Oxford, Milton Keynes and Bedford are in now hand by East West Rail, together with plans for the longer-term restoration back to Cambridge, making the line a useful part of any future London orbital railway.

The end of the national passenger network at Okehampton, viewed in June 2016. The heritage Dartmoor Railway continues on to Meldon, whilst the station, after some years of passenger closure, is currently served once again on summer Sundays. Plans to reopen the ex-LSWR route on to Plymouth, which closed in May 1968, as an alternative to the coastal line at Dawlish, have been considered. *Author*

# The South Western Main Line via Okehampton

The 60-mile ex-LSWR line was open throughout by 1876, although it was 1891 before all aspects of the double-track main line were complete. The Beeching Report indicated that the Exeter–Okehampton section conveyed more passengers than the line to Barnstaple and therefore this section was never considered for closure. As for individual stations on the route, the Beeching Report also showed passenger receipts at Lydford, Tavistock and Okehampton as being amongst some of the busiest in the area. The Okehampton–

Plymouth section was proposed for closure simply because the entire route was seen to duplicate the coastal line via Dawlish.

Again after a fight, this main line, once used by the 'Atlantic Coast Express', was closed as a through route in May 1968. The 23-mile central section has closed completely, with part now being used by the Granite Way footpath and cycleway. There have been calls for its reopening as it would add several important settlements to the national passenger network. In particular, reopening would add resilience to the wider South West railway network, acting as the most sensible diversionary route to the winter storm-prone coastal line via Dawlish.

## The Midland main line through the Peak District

The ex-MR Derby–Manchester Central route was built through the stunning limestone scenery of the Derbyshire Peak District; the steep sided valleys sometimes being known as 'Little Switzerland'. Opening in 1863, the 61-mile, double-track main line had fine viaducts and many tunnels. It also had a number of attractive station buildings. In later years it was used as a diversionary route to the WCML between London and Manchester, with busy passenger and freight use. 'Britannia' class locomotives and the Blue Midland Pullman could be seen on the line.

Dr Beeching never even recommended this line for closure, but one of the shocks of his Report was that the line to Buxton was recommended for closure; fortunately sanity prevailed and Buxton is still open. However, this busy main line was closed to remaining express services in July 1968. Local lines, the Peak Rail heritage railway and the Monsal Trail now use much of the former route, and reopening of the remaining 15-mile closed section between Great Rocks and Rowsley looks increasingly complex.

## Some losses in Scotland

This 23-mile, double-track ex-NBR Cowdenbeath–Kinross Junction–Bridge of Earn line provided the shortest route from Perth and the Highlands to and from Edinburgh. Again, this well used line was not even proposed for closure in the Beeching Report. Indeed, in 1967 it was included as part of the Network for Development. Yet it was controversially closed in January 1970 for reasons at the time that were not clear. The emergence a little later of the M90 motorway on part of the trackbed is a significant clue to the likely demise of this route. There have been calls for reopening of this most notorious closure of a main line, but the reopening of a nearby single line freight route to passengers has helped provide a slightly more direct Edinburgh–Perth route.

To the north east of Perth the 44-mile ex-CR Stanley Junction–Kinnaber Junction line, via Forfar in the Vale of Strathmore, was another double-track main line that was proposed for closure in the Beeching Report. It seemingly duplicated a different route running via the coast. The line was once associated with the last leg of the rival East and West Coast Express trains that competed between London and Aberdeen. Mostly suited for high-speed running, it was closed simply on the basis of duplication and main line trains to and from

Millers Dale in the Peak District, on the ex-MR main Derby–Manchester line, was once an important junction for Buxton, until the closure of all such intermediate stations in March 1967, prior to complete closure. One of the huge viaducts built here is seen in September 1993. Only a relatively short section of line would have to reopen to restore the Derby–Manchester route through here. *Author*

The line through the Vale of Strathmore in Scotland was once a high-speed section on the London–Aberdeen route. Coupar Angus is seen in September 1983. Passenger traffic was diverted via Dundee in September 1967 and the former CR main line ended up as a freight-only branch, closing in June 1982. *Author*

The Stanley Junction–Kinnaber Junction section of main line ran through many small stations. Woodside & Burrelton signal box, with stacked sleepers in front, is recorded in September 1983, after complete closure of the route the previous year. A small section of line at Bridge of Dun has been restored as part of the heritage Caledonian Railway. *Author*

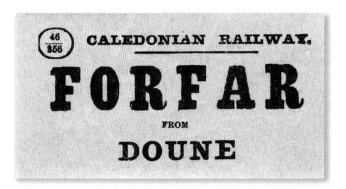

Aberdeen were diverted off the route in September 1967.

The 71-mile Stranraer–Dumfries line ran through a remote and rugged part of Scotland and some of the engineering structures on this route are illustrated elsewhere in this book. Apart from serving important small towns, the line developed as one of the main links to Northern Ireland. It became known as the 'Port Road' as boat trains and through sleeping cars to and from London provided important connecting ferry traffic. When closure of most of the line was recommended in the Beeching Report there was an outcry, yet the diversion of London-Stranraer trains via Ayr finally put paid to the line which closed in June 1965.

## North to Northallerton

The 28¼-mile, double-track Harrogate–Northallerton route developed as a main line from Leeds and Harrogate to the north via Ripon. Opened in 1848, it became part of the NER in 1854. The LNER in particular promoted Ripon, with its cathedral, racecourse and nearby Fountains Abbey, as a tourist destination. Ripon also developed as a calling point on Anglo-Scottish Pullman services and such was the importance of the line that works were carried out at Northallerton during World War 2 to ensure the resilience of the route.

The busy line was identified in the Beeching Report for closure and, in 1964, main line trains were diverted off the route and the line closed in March 1967. However, an accident on the ECML saw its use as a diversionary route for a few days later that summer. Remaining track was removed in 1970. There have been for many years moves to reopen the line and provide a new station at Ripon, the track once again acting as a diversionary route for the ECML.

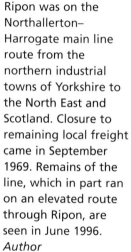

Ripon was on the Northallerton–Harrogate main line route from the northern industrial towns of Yorkshire to the North East and Scotland. Closure to remaining local freight came in September 1969. Remains of the line, which in part ran on an elevated route through Ripon, are seen in June 1996. *Author*

The later rebuilt station at Ripon was designed so as the entrance, with its three arches, loosely reflected the cathedral entrance. The station once provided a refreshment room and for a time the NER operated a bus to the cathedral and marketplace. The buildings were in residential use when this view was taken in June 1996. *Author*

## The Great Central Main Line

The foremost main line to have been lost in England was the ex-GCR route from London Marylebone running along over 200 miles of double-track to Sheffield and Manchester. The London extension opening in 1899 was built with no major road crossings, slight gradients and broad curves for high-speed running. Much of the line was also built so it could, if required, accommodate the larger continental loading gauge as the original visionary plan was for trains to run all the way to France via a Channel Tunnel. Even under BR in the 1950s the Sheffield–Manchester section was electrified and a new three-mile tunnel built under the Pennines.

It was the last main line to reach London, but this modern and well-built railway was seen simply as a duplicating route by Dr Beeching. The route was transferred from the ER to the LMR in 1958 and express Manchester–Marylebone services were withdrawn soon after. It closed as a main line between 1966 and May 1969, with large parts being abandoned. The heritage Great Central Railway run a section from the north of Leicester to the south of Nottingham, suburban services run from London Marylebone to Aylesbury and some other short sections of line remain open. Being substantially built, many remains of the closed sections can still be seen.

The GCR's London Extension was the last main line built during the Victorian period. Rugby Central station is seen in January 1994. Regretfully, much of the Manchester–Aylesbury section was closed by May 1969, the largest single closure of the Beeching era. *Author*

BR poster promoting the Manchester–Sheffield main line in 1955, with artwork by V. Welch. Sadly, after so much investment, including a new tunnel over 3 miles in length, completed in 1953 at a cost of about £4.25 million (multiply this by about 25 to get a very approximate cost in 2018 terms), the line was closed to remaining traffic in July 1981. *NRM/Science & Society Picture Library*

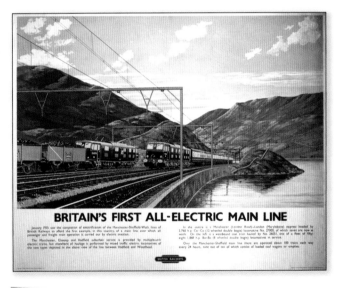

## The Somerset & Dorset Joint Railway

The 63¾-mile Broadstone Junction–Bath Green Park S&D main line became something of a legend in its own lifetime and was the best loved of the joint lines. It was created by amalgamations in 1862 and had remained outside the Grouping in 1923, but its joint days ended with nationalisation in 1948. The line developed to become a very distinctive and evocative railway, particularly the image of holiday trains struggling on the steep gradients over the scenic Mendip Hills to and from the south coast.

Much of the passenger traffic was seasonal and, apart from the 'Pines Express', long-distance passenger trains to and from the north of England eventually only ran during the summer. The main line railway linked Bournemouth West and Poole with Bath Green Park. There were also several important towns on its route. Under BR, the line was transferred from the Southern Region to the Western Region. The new regime seemed intent on running the railway down and passenger services on the line ceased in

March 1966, with all remaining freight sections having closed by September 1973. Parts are now used as cycleways and footpaths, but such have been the emotions stirred by this evocative railway that ambitions for a revival have resulted in some short sections, for the present, being reopened as heritage railways.

The ex-S&D route contained considerable lengths of single-line, such as this near Bath, seen in March 2009. The 'Pines Express' was, until it was diverted off the line in 1962, the most famous train using the heavily-graded route over the Mendips between Bath Green Park and Bournemouth West. Closure of the route to passengers came in March 1966. *Author*

## Ruabon–Barmouth

The 53¼-mile ex-GWR through route in North Wales from Ruabon to the Cambrian Coast at Barmouth Junction, now Morfa Mawddach, was opened in 1869. It was always shown on GWR and BR maps as a main line. Passenger traffic built up, particularly during the summer and prior to World War 1. As a consequence, the Ruabon–Llangollen section was doubled in 1900 and additional passing loops were added to the remaining single-line. Travelling through glorious Welsh countryside, it served a number of important small towns. After World War 2, traffic declined, but summer excursion trains were still busy.

Evidence shows that even though this well used line was identified in the Beeching Report for closure, this was only very reluctantly agreed to as it isolated a number of

important Welsh towns. Yet once again only one line could run to the Cambrian Coast; it was seen at the time to duplicate the line via Welshpool. It was closed to passengers in January 1965 and remaining freight ceased in April 1968. The Llangollen–Corwen section has reopened as a heritage railway and it is hoped one day this line may extend back to Ruabon. The Bala Lake narrow-gauge line also runs on part of the old trackbed.

Llangollen was a busy intermediate stop on the ex-GWR Ruabon–Barmouth Junction line and is now on a heritage railway that uses part of the route as far as Corwen. It is said there was real upset at the closure of this line to passengers in January 1965, which served several important Welsh settlements. The restored station is seen in September 2003. *Author*

Firsby was once a busy junction for Skegness on the ex-GNR Grimsby–Peterborough main line, viewed here in September 1964. Trains were diverted off the route which was downgraded to that of a branch line, before closure of key sections in October 1970. The Grimsby–Louth freight service survived until December 1980. *Author*

# The East Lincolnshire Main Line

The ex-GNR 78-mile, double-track Peterborough–Grimsby line was opened in sections by 1886. It contained long stretches of straight line and developed as a main route that during the peak summer period was very busy, with excursions to Skegness and other Lincolnshire coastal destinations. Until 1964 fish was an important freight running from Grimsby to London, whilst there was once also significant agricultural freight. DMUs were introduced for local services in 1955, but few other economies were made on this line which ran through a flat area of Lincolnshire, with lots of manually operated level crossings. A lengthy enquiry into closure took place at Skegness, but diversions off the line and service reductions had already been made and after a fight the line closed in October 1970.

The Boston–Skegness section was reprieved on the basis that there were poor roads and this was an isolated area. The 16-mile Spalding–Peterborough section subsequently reopened in 1971 and the Lincolnshire Wolds heritage railway runs on a section to the north of Louth.

Louth was one of the most attractive stations on the GNR; the beautiful Jacobean styled buildings were stately home in nature. They fell into disrepair after passenger services ceased in 1970, but freight to adjoining maltings continued for over a decade. This view, taken in September 1994, shows restoration for residential use underway. *Author*

# 17
# Urban remains

Railways represented the greatest works of the Victorian age and from an architectural viewpoint, Victorian railway buildings were as good as any public building of their time. Sadly, the closure of railways in the 'swinging sixties' coincided with a short-sighted modernism movement that was all for sweeping away Victorian buildings at that time.

Many beautiful Victorian railway buildings in urban areas were lost, often to what now looks to be poor-quality new development, some of which has since been torn down. In a number of cases, urban land values simply overrode any respect for the buildings. Examples of large termini that have been both closed and sadly demolished include the outstanding Glasgow St Enoch, Dundee West, Nottingham Victoria and Birkenhead Woodside stations. Birmingham Snow Hill, Crystal Palace High Level, Sheffield Victoria and London Broad Street were also big losses. Leeds and Liverpool Central stations, Yarmouth South Town, Bradford Adolphus Street, Stockport Tiviot Dale and Fleetwood were other once distinctive urban stations that have all but disappeared.

Birkenhead Woodside opened in 1878 and when seen in September 2007, only some stone capped walls remained of this once splendid GW & LNW Joint station. It was the most northerly station served by GWR passenger trains. The preserved metal station gates are also to be found on the Wirral. Closed in November 1967, the terminus was demolished within two years. *Author*

Sheffield Victoria station closed in January 1970 and was mostly demolished by 1989, but these steps to a side entrance survived in September 1994 and the location can still be identified today. The sealed-up door in the top left was once the entrance to a passenger lift, accessed via a metal walkway. A charge of one old penny was made for the lift service. *Author*

There are, however, a number of isolated railway remains in urban areas with some being such treasures that they have defied the demolition teams. Railway statues and war memorials apart, their survival has, for the most part, been rather hit and miss. By way of example, stone gate houses survive at Euston inscribed with some destinations that are no longer served by train. The Glasgow Subway entrance building at St Enoch, a MR water tower outside St Pancras and Mersey Railway pumping station buildings all survive. The beautiful red and white brickwork at Crystal Palace High Level pedestrian subway remains. The quality and design are both such that this is certainly a sunken railway treasure.

In London, the triumphal stone Doric Euston Arch was demolished simply on the sacrificial altar of modernity, even the demolition contractor offered to store it for free. The shocking loss was seen as a turning point in the ever-more destructive behaviour of the time. Shortly after, the demolition was also proposed of St Pancras, but the outcry caused by the Euston Arch helped prevent a similar catastrophe. Fortunately, at the other end of the London & Birmingham Railway, Curzon Street station buildings also survived. The remaining stone building was once a hotel and is to be incorporated into the proposed new HS2 terminal at Birmingham. As the world's earliest surviving piece of monumental railway architecture, it is also one of my top 10 closed railway treasures.

*Right:* Crystal Palace burnt down in 1936, removing much traffic from the line that directly served the venue, although the ex-SECR High Level station did not close until September 1954. The subway, dating from 1865, was intended for first class ticket holders. Although the main station buildings have been demolished, the fan-vaulted brick subway remains and is seen in May 1995. *Author*

*Opposite:* Bradford Exchange closed in January 1973 and most of the station, which had become rather dilapidated, was demolished by 1976. The large scale of the 10-platformed ex-LY & GN Joint station is apparent from this view which shows part of a stone retaining wall dating from the station rebuilding of 1880 and seen in April 1996. *Author*

*Left:* Edinburgh Murrayfield, with a bridge abutment, viewed in June 2011, that supported an equally ornamental metal bridge, was on the ex-CR Edinburgh Princes Street–Leith service. Opened in 1879 and closed to passengers in April 1962, freight ceased in September 1967. Princes Street station closed in September 1965. *Author*

*Below:* Glasgow Clydebank Riverside station, the hexagonal tower in brick and sandstone, represents the prosperity of this shipbuilding area when it was opened in 1896. After closure in October 1964 there was a period of dereliction before the building was converted into residential use. It is viewed in October 2011. *Author*

Glasgow Kelvinside was opened by the CR in 1896 and a stone monogram of the railway can still be found here. The elegant sandstone building was built to an Italianate Renaissance style. It was closed to passengers by the LMS in July 1942, but the building survives as a restaurant and is seen in September 2009. *Author*

Gosport station's impressive colonnade, dating from 1841, is in contrast to some more functional LSWR stations. The station lost its roof during a World War 2 air raid. Passenger traffic ended in June 1953 and freight in January 1969. The picture was taken in September 1995, but the building has since been restored and put into residential use. *Author*

Oxford for many years had a LNWR station called Oxford Rewley Road. This closed in October 1951 and became dilapidated, as a view of part of the station roof seen in September 1989 shows. Built in 1851 by the same contractor as the Crystal Palace, the station was also capable of being dismantled. It was eventually re-sited and restored at the Buckinghamshire Railway Centre. *Author*

Birmingham Curzon Street, with the crest of the London & Birmingham Railway, seen in August 2001. The impressive stone building was designed by Phillip Hardwick, opening in 1838. Closed to regular passengers in 1854, when a new through station was built, lines remained for freight until January 1966. The area is now the future location for a new HS2 station. *Author*

Leeds station has a spacious north concourse built by the LMS in 1937–8 to provide a pedestrian route from the Queens Hotel and existing station to the former Wellington station. When this view was taken in April 1966, the lofty hallway was used for parking. Shops now occupy the entrances to the closed Wellington platforms and the concourse has been refurbished for pedestrian use. *Author*

Leicester Central station was opened by the GCR in 1899 and parts still exist, including the original ridge and furrow glass roof of the taxi waiting entrance to the station, which is seen in September 2016. The station was eventually reduced to almost an unstaffed halt and closed in May 1969, together with much of the remaining ex-GCR line. *Author*

Liverpool Exchange station was extended by the LYR in 1870, but the remaining frontage dates from 1888. The Southport line was proposed for closure, but was reprieved and trains diverted to other stations at Liverpool. Exchange station closed in April 1977 and the iron train sheds were demolished soon after. The free Renaissance-style former hotel frontage and clock, seen in April 2006, remain and are now offices. *Author*

Where urban station buildings do endure they are sometimes in a modified form. Only the frontage of Liverpool Exchange remains, whilst Edinburgh Princes Street and Leith Central station train sheds have been demolished. Businesses are found in many locations in arches under disused viaducts from those proposed under the Braithwaite Viaduct in London, to those under the remaining St Enoch Viaduct in Glasgow. Urban parks have been proposed on the top of disused viaducts at Leeds Holbeck, Peckham and Camden, whilst others have been used as footpaths and cycleways.

An ex-MR closed station with much remaining is Manchester Central with its train shed, now used as a conference centre, sitting above a labyrinth of subterranean arches and next to the Midland Hotel. The massive passenger station is top of my top 10 closed railway treasures. In contrast to this huge building, the smaller Manchester Liverpool Road station also remains. Dating from 1830, it is the oldest surviving purpose-built urban station in Britain and as such, with the adjoining railway buildings now a museum, is also one of my top 10 closed railway treasures.

The stone-built Bristol Old Terminus, designed by I. K. Brunel with an amazing wood and iron hammer-beam styled roof, dating back to 1839, is moreover one of my top 10 closed railway treasures. The nearby Bristol & Exeter buildings, dating from 1845, also survive and show that age is no bar to urban survival. Other treasures are still to be found, the stone built Green Park terminus at Bath, which has been put to good new use, together with the distinctive London Road station at Nottingham. At Wolverhampton, the Queen's Building from the original station in yellow bricks contrasts with the closed Low Level station, an example of a blue engineering brick built GWR station, demonstrating the variety of styles and materials used in urban areas.

Manchester Central station in August 2016. The huge train shed span was 210ft (64m) wide and reached a height of 90ft (27m). Closure on 5 May 1969 was announced with special BR posters. After a period of dereliction, the station was renovated and a time capsule dating from the 1880 opening was found. The magnificent train shed remains and is now used as a conference centre. *Author*

Wonderful former railway hotels apart, hidden away in urban areas can be found a number of closed station treasures, for example such as those in a classical style at Gosport, Leith Citadel, Lincoln St Marks, Monkwearmouth and Southampton's original terminus station. The remains often provide an indication to the changing economic fortunes of areas, for example, the fine railway buildings at Clydebank Riverside hark back to the days when Glasgow was the second city of Empire and this was a wealthy shipbuilding area.

In London, a number of railway buildings have been lost due to bomb damage in World War 2. The railway hotels at Holborn Viaduct, London Bridge and Cannon Street were all destroyed. The London Necropolis Railway was opened in 1854 and over 2,000 bodies were carried each year. The London station was severely damaged in the Blitz and funeral trains never ran again, but the station frontage still survives.

Bristol Old Station was a masterpiece for its time. Designed in 1839 by I. K. Brunel, the GWR station boasted of a unique wood and iron Tudor-styled hammer-beam roof, with a span of 72ft (22m). Since September 1965 it has not been part of the operational station, whilst in 1970 access was blocked by a new signal box. The roof is pictured in June 1993. *Author*

*Right:* Bath Green Park was elegantly designed in Bath stone to complement Bath itself. It was opened in 1870 by the MR. Today parking and retail uses are to be found beneath the main 66ft (20m) vaulted wrought iron ribbed roof, together with two side spans giving a total 110ft (34m) width. The interior is observed in June 1993, passenger trains having ceased in March 1966. *Author*

*Below:* Summer excursions from Bath in 1902.

| EVERY SATURDAY during JULY, AUGUST & SEPTEMBER, A Cheap Excursion Train will leave BATH (Mid. station) at 1.30 p.m. for | | | |
|---|---|---|---|
| STATIONS. | RETURN FARE. Third Class. | STATIONS. | RETURN FARE. Third Class. |
| RADSTOCK Midsomer Norton and Welton Chilcompton | **1s. 3d.** | SHEPTON MALLET Evercreech New | **1s. 9d.** |
| Binegar, Masbury | **1s. 6d.** | Evercreech Junction | |

Wolverhampton Low Level was completed in 1855 by the GWR and the classical design in blue engineering bricks is unique. The Brunel-designed overall roof was demolished in 1933 and passenger traffic ceased in March 1972. The station became a parcels concentration depot in 1970, but all traffic ended in June 1981. After a period of dereliction, as noted in August 2000, the main building was restored to new uses. *Author*

Wolverhampton Low Level departures April 1956.

| Another Route LOW LEVEL STATION. REFRESHMENT ROOMS. From Paddington.  Same fares. | | | |
|---|---|---|---|
| Padd. a.m. | Wolv. | Wolv. a.m. | Padd. |
| 12  5 | 4 15 | 12 20c¶ | 5 10 |
| 7 10 | 10 57 | 6 45 | 10  5 |
| 9  0er | 11 30 | 7 25er | 10 17 |
| 9 10r | 12  5 | 8 35r | 11 10 |
| 10 10r | 12 37 | 9 35 | 12 15 |
| 11 10r | 1 42 | 11 35er | 2 15 |
| p.m. | | 11 35sr | 2 22 |
| 2 10r | 4 57 | p.m. | |
| 4 10r | 7 10 | 2 35r | 5 15 |
| 5 10er | 7 56 | 3 35r | 6  7 |
| 6 10r | 9 16 | 4 35er | 7 15 |
| 7 10h | 10 13 | 5 20f | 8 20 |
| 7 35sr | 11 27 | 5 33r | 8 35 |
| 7 35er | 11 32 | 7 30hr | 10 15 |
| — | — | 7 30kr | 11 30 |

Leith had several stations and North Leith dating from 1846, also called Leith Citadel, was designed by Grainger & Miller in a classical style. Columns decorated with acanthus leaves and harebells were provided and one of the capitals is seen here in June 2011. The station was closed for passengers by the LNER in June 1947, but freight survived until February 1968. *Author*

Southampton Terminus station in May 1995. The original southern terminal of the London & Southampton Railway, opened in 1840 and closed to passengers in September 1966, had been greatly extended over the years, as seen here. At the London end the railway originally terminated at Nine Elms, with the journey to Waterloo being completed by boat. *Author*

Staines West was opened in 1885 by the GWR. Looking rather unlike any other GWR station was due to the fact that the railway bought an existing dignified Georgian dwelling and converted it into to a station. The line closed to all traffic in March 1965. The building is seen in September 1997. *Author*

*Opposite:* Monkwearmouth lies north of Sunderland and a grand station was opened in 1848 by George Hudson, to celebrate him becoming the local MP. The station closed to passengers in March 1967 and eventually became a railway museum, but this has since closed. The imposing stone ionic column portico is seen in October 2016. *Author*

London's cemeteries became full and railways were used to convey the dead to cemeteries outside the city. The most famous was the London Necropolis Railway, running its own trains to Brookwood Cemetery in Surrey. The London Waterloo station frontage is pictured in April 2015. Although repaired from World War 2 damage, this did result in the termination of all services from April 1941. *Author*

A number of urban former railway freight buildings remain throughout Britain. Many were huge, functional brick structures and the ex-GNR warehouses at Manchester Deansgate and King's Cross are particularly imposing. Several buildings have found new economic uses many years after closure. Others have been demolished, including the curved edifice of the ex-LNWR warehouse at Oldham in 2012.

The railways brought about unified time for clocks in Britain and showpiece clock towers were sometimes provided at major stations, both as an urban landmark and to assist passenger punctuality. The closed stations at Tunbridge Wells West, Southport Lord Street and Leith Central all retain their clock towers. The huge station clock tower at Nottingham is all that remains of the Victoria station, but it is so imposing and attractive that it is included as one of my top 10 closed railway treasures.

**Aldwych Service**

FROM HOLBORN
Weekdays only—
First train 6.15 a.m.
Last train 11.55 p.m.

FROM ALDWYCH.
Weekdays only—
First train 6.18 a.m.
Last train 11.58 p.m.

Journey time, 1 min.
Trains every 5 min.

Aldwych timetable April 1956.

London Underground had many stations designed by Leslie Green. His use of maroon glazed terracotta tiles was a masterpiece of creative design as they withstood staining by the weather and pollutants. The distinctive looks also made London tube stations instantly recognisable. This 1907 façade at Aldwych was of a slightly different design and is seen on the day of its final closure in September 1994. *Author*

Derby Roundhouse MR offices led to the locomotive roundhouse itself, which dates from 1839 and is the earliest in the country. An additional floor was added later to the office building reducing slightly the impact of the stone clock tower. Disused by 1988 and narrowly escaping demolition, the restored buildings, seen in September 2016, are now part of Derby College. *Author*

On my travels over the years many disused urban railway buildings have attracted both my admiration and interest. A selection of my personal favourites are illustrated in this chapter.

*Below right:* London's earliest roundhouse engine shed was built at Camden in 1846–7. It could house 24 locomotives around a central turntable, but by the 1860s became obsolete as the size of locomotives increased. In 1869 it was used as a gin warehouse and in 1964 was converted for use as a cultural centre. It is seen in September 1997 and is now a concert venue. *Author*

*Below:* Swindon Works were first operational in 1843 and once covered a huge area, but went into decline when locomotive production ceased. *Evening Star*, the last steam engine built by BR in 1960, was made here and the works closed in March 1986. Many of the buildings have been retained in new uses, but some other buildings were in various states of disrepair such as this seen in June 1993. *Author*

Southport Lord Street station opened in 1884 and closed in July 1952. Although the train shed was demolished, the Southport & Cheshire Lines Extension Railway's grand clock tower of the five-platformed terminus remains. The building, now a hotel, remains a useful and distinguished part of the seaside town and is seen in April 2006. *Author*

Nottingham Victoria station clock tower, viewed in January 2008. The red brick and Darley Dale stone Baroque Revival styled tower, dating from 1900, was saved when the rest of the station was demolished, just days after closure in September 1967. The clock had been stopped before closure, which added to the desolation of the station, but today the correct time is shown. *Author*

Tunbridge Wells West was opened in 1866 by the LBSCR who wanted to make a statement against incursions of the SER. As a consequence, a clock tower graces the former station and it was even sometimes known as the 'St Pancras of the Weald'. The station closed in July 1985 and is seen here in July 1989. The Spa Valley Railway use part of the station site and the building remains. *Author*

# 18
# Ports and piers

Bradshaw's Railway Guide for 1910 indicated that you could travel to almost anywhere in the world by ship and train from rail-served British ports. At home many of the pre-Grouping railway companies had their own ports, marine stations and ships. The LYR had 28 ships, the largest of the pre-Grouping fleets, whilst the GWR became the largest dock-owning company.

The ships were taken over by the Big Four in 1923 and the LMS owned 66 in 1939. Many were later requisitioned and destroyed during World War 2, including those sunk during the evacuation of Dunkirk. Nevertheless, in 1948 the ports were nationalised and BR inherited over 100 ships ranging from train ferries to small river ferryboats. In 1981 the railway ports were sold off and, three years later, the remaining railway shipping fleet was also disposed of to private operators.

Yet there were railway-served ports that never quite made it. By way of some examples, in 1856 silting up made Port Carlisle increasingly difficult to reach, just two years after the railway to that port had opened. Portpatrick Harbour closed for services to Ireland in 1874. Its exposed quays were not ideal in stormy weather and ships were transferred to a more sheltered Stranraer, where ferry services continued until 2011. The irregular Burnham–South Wales passenger services ceased in 1888. The inland Fort Augustus Pier–Inverness service, using Loch Ness, last operated in 1906 after the rival HR main line to Inverness had been improved. The railway to Tollesbury Pier closed in 1921 and to Southwold Harbour in 1929; both were originally considered good port locations, but silting up contributed to their demise as commercial ports.

Rusting narrow-gauge track in the mud on the bank of the River Blyth at Southwold Harbour, seen in June 1999. The harbour branch was opened in 1914, just as World War 1 curtailed the North Sea fishing industry. Coastal trade was slow to recover and the branch closed in April 1929. After only 15 years of use, this track had remained disused for many more years. *Author*

Burnham-on-Sea in Somerset with silted-up remains of the railway pier, seen in March 2009. Instigated by George Reed, a director of the local railway, it was once advertised as a 'Gateway to the Continent' as its links to Poole allowed connections to Le Havre. It was not successful and use declined in the 1880s, although pleasure steamers used Burnham until World War 1. *Author*

At one time, all ports of any significance were served by railways and several ports provided their own lines and locomotives. On the freight side many ports have lost their railway connections. Coal is no longer exported from Britain in any significant quantity and this has led to a sharp decrease in a number of coal ports. Methil was once the largest coal exporting port in Scotland, but ceased this trade in 1977 and was subsequently reduced in size. The same was the case in South Wales. Newport once had over 100 miles of coal sidings, Cardiff saw the last coal train in 1964, Barry in 1976 and Swansea in 1987, but as with many former coal ports, they remain in use with other freight.

*Below:* Beckton Gas Works was located on the River Thames and at one time was the largest gas works in the world, with an extensive network of 70 miles of internal lines. The last train left the works in June 1970. The huge legs of the river pier are difficult to remove and may just be left, as can be seen in September 2014. *Author*

Ranleigh Road level crossing in September 2011, leading to Ipswich Docks. LNER gate lamps converted to electric lighting remained on this section of the line. The dock branch was officially closed in March 2012, after several years of being out of use. Ipswich Docks continues to be rail served at Griffin Wharf. *Author*

The train ferry gantry still survives at Harwich and is pictured in November 2012. Originally built in 1916 for World War 1 use, it was re-erected at Harwich by the LNER in 1923. By means of a hinged section of railway track, it allowed rail wagons to board ships at any state of the tide. It closed in January 1987. *Author*

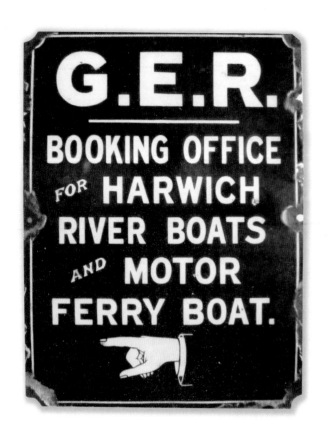

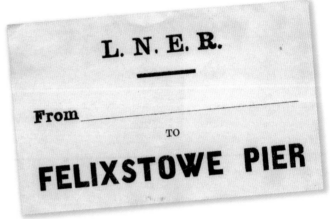

Dunston Staithes are located in the River Tyne. Completed in 1903 by the NER, coal mined in the area was loaded directly into ships from wagons on the staithes. Being 66ft (20m) high and 1,725ft (526m) long, it is the largest wooden structure in Europe. Closed in March 1980 and damaged by fire in 2003, the staithes are pictured in October 2016. *Author*

Heysham was a key MR port for the Isle of Man and Ireland. The once extensive station was in the process of being reduced in size and the canopies removed when seen here in September 1993. The terminus closed in October 1975, but limited services resumed to a small part of the station in May 1987. *Author*

The GWR warehouses at Liverpool's Manchester Dock were designed to receive barge cargoes from Morpeth Docks in Birkenhead. The GWR service ceased in the 1920s; the view was taken in July 2000 and the preserved buildings still remain. A Birkenhead–Liverpool passenger ferry also ran and the Mersey Ferry still operates. *Author*

Some ports, after years of use, have closed as commercial harbours altogether. Whitstable Harbour, the first railway harbour in the world, had fallen into disuse and closed in 1952. Slate exports from Porthmadog Harbour ended in 1946, whilst at Port Dinorwic, now Y Felinheli, slate was exported until 1961. Lydney Harbour closed to freight in 1977 and the last coal train ran to Burry Port as late as 1996. As with many other smaller former commercial harbours, they have since developed as marinas.

The PLA once ran a network of 140 miles of line, but the last London Docks closed in 1980, replaced by docks capable of handling larger ships downriver at Tilbury. A similar situation at Bristol Harbour resulted in the expansion of Avonmouth. Salford Docks on the Manchester Ship Canal closed in 1982. Many ports have seen the redevelopment of surplus dock facilities, whilst other ports that remain open have lost their quayside railway links.

The Silvertown Tramway in London's docklands provided one of the closest level crossings to central London. Closure of the remaining line came in 1985 and the crossing is viewed here in September 1997. Nearby the new Crossrail uses the old Connaught Tunnel on a section of the closed North Woolwich line. The Tate & Lyle building is on the right. *Author*

The Thames ferry crossing at North Woolwich Pier was closed by the GER in 1908, a few years after the nearby free ferry opened. The pier remained in use for paddle steamer excursions until the 1950s. The North Woolwich station terminus in the background closed in December 2006 and is seen, with the remains of the pier, in September 2014. *Author*

A complex network of lines was developed by the LSWR and later SR at Southampton Docks. Even now an occasional steam excursion can access some of the dock lines to serve cruise liners, although the number of such trains is much diminished. Bulleid Pacific *Clan Line*, No 35028, is seen having arrived at Southampton with 'The Cunarder' in May 1995. *Author*

On the passenger side, the development of transatlantic crossings had seen the *Titanic* depart from Southampton, with passengers passing through the original LSWR terminal to board the fateful journey. This terminal was later extended by the SR, but closed in September 1966. The buildings still survive, whilst a new Ocean Terminal, which provided a short step from Southampton boat trains to the transatlantic liners and opened in 1950, was mostly demolished in 1983. This modern structure was short-lived as transatlantic traffic went increasingly by air from the 1950s.

Liverpool was once a key transatlantic passenger port and trains ran to the Riverside terminus to connect with ocean liners. Cunard services ended in 1966 and the station closed in February 1971, but here the Mersey Ferry *Woodchurch* approaches the *Queen Elizabeth 2* in mid-channel at Liverpool in July 1990. The *QE2* was laid up in 2009. *Author*

Liverpool's Riverside terminus opened in 1895 and was used as the departure point for transatlantic crossings. Boat trains once served this station from London and a number of northern cities. It was also used for some services to the Isle of Man and Ireland. All the ports were busy during World War 2; no fewer than 4,648 troop trains used the Riverside station during this period. Regular transatlantic crossings to and from Liverpool ended in 1968, the station closed in February 1971 and was demolished in 1990.

Scotland's transatlantic services ran from Greenock and a new Princes Pier station opened here in 1894. Regular passenger services ended in February 1959, but boat trains remained to and from Glasgow, with the last one running in November 1965. Freight continued until Princes Pier station closed in September 1966 and the station was demolished in 1967. In 1971 a container terminal opened on the site, although its connecting line has been out of use since 1991.

Birkenhead at one time had a network of railway lines serving the docks. Flexibility was provided by wagon turntables as they saved space on providing points in confined areas and also allowed stock with doors on just a single side to be turned. The turntable diameter was slightly larger than the wheelbase of the four-wheeled wagons and one is seen in September 2006. *Author*

*Above:* Dover Marine, renamed Dover Western Docks in 1979, was a huge terminus built on reclaimed land. It was a key departure port for Europe before the Channel Tunnel opened in May 1994. The steel train shed provided shelter from the elements. The terminus is seen in September 1994, just prior to passenger closure. *Author*

*Left:* Folkestone Harbour and other south coast ports were used extensively during both World Wars to ferry troops and equipment to and from France, for the war effort. The harbour station was closed to regular passengers in 2001, but was used by Pullman excursions before formal closure in July 2014. The band for such a Pullman train arrival is seen here in May 2009. *Author*

The opening of the Channel Tunnel in 1994 had implications for nearby ports. Dover Marine, later renamed Western Docks, was the largest maritime railway station in Britain, opening at the end of World War 1 it was once the main gateway to the continent. 'The Golden Arrow' used the station until 1972 and 'The Night Ferry' until 1980. The station closed in 1994, but fortunately the building was saved and converted into a cruise terminal. At neighbouring Folkestone Harbour the station was rebuilt by 1856 and, as with other south coast ports, saw heavy usage in both world wars. Although not used for regular passenger services since 2001, British Pullman excursion trains ran until 2009. The station was officially closed in 2014 and has been incorporated into a new walkway using the closed line.

EMU stock being hauled by a Class 33/1 push-pull diesel with a boat train from Waterloo, in September 1983. The train is making its way along Commercial Road to Weymouth Quay, for a connecting ship to the Channel Islands. Last used in 1999, the tramway at Weymouth was officially closed in 2016. *Author*

Gravesend West station led to a Thames pier on two levels. Shelter for the platforms leading to the pier was rather rudimentary with corrugated asbestos sheets. Passenger services ended in August 1953 and remaining freight traffic in March 1968. This view, taken in April 1995, was before demolition of the station in 2006, but the river pier still remains. *Author*

Weymouth Quay was connected by a street tramway to the main line station that enabled boat trains to run direct from Waterloo to the quayside. Opened in 1865, the tramway was last used for regular boat trains connecting to ships for the Channel Islands in September 1987. Although use continued until 1999 and it was still *in situ* in 2017, it was officially closed in 2016.

Gravesend and Tilbury competed for European traffic. Gravesend West station was located on a pier and served by boat trains from London Victoria, but these ended in 1953 and the station closed in 1968. On the north bank of the Thames, Tilbury Riverside station had a direct rail route to London Fenchurch Street, but passenger use declined and it closed in 1992. The imposing buildings remain and the floating pontoon is still used by cruise ships.

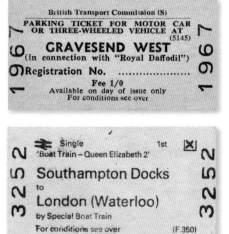

The very first railway ferry passenger service opened in 1848 between New Holland Pier and Hull Corporation Pier. The service was withdrawn in 1981 after the Humber Bridge was opened. However, two of the ex-LNER Humber paddle steamer ferries, *Tattershall Castle* and *Wingfield Castle*, are still in existence.

A network of railway steamer routes provided many connections to coastal towns and resorts. The preserved *Waverley*, an ex-LNER paddle steamer, even now plies the Clyde and other ports in the summer. However, connections with the tramway at Rothesay and narrow-gauge railway at Campbeltown have not been available since their closures in the 1930s.

Two islands with significant railway networks served from British mainland ports were particularly busy in summer.

The LMS and PLA rebuilt Tilbury Riverside by 1930. It provided a floating landing stage that enabled ships to berth at any state of the tide. The station closed in November 1992 and an entrance is seen in December 1997. The main terminal building remains, as does the floating landing stage, whilst a passenger ferry to Gravesend and cruise ships still use the landing stage. *Author*

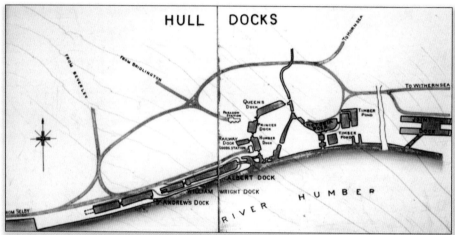

Hull Docks were shown as an inset map on NER tile maps. A number of these historic maps still remain. The Hull Dock Company and the NER merged in 1893. This rather simplified map ignores the fact that rival HB railway dock lines were also in operation at this time. Although many lines are closed, Hull Docks remain rail served. *Author*

New Holland Pier–Hull Corporation Pier ferry services closed in June 1981, once the Humber road bridge opened. When this view was taken in August 1994, much of the track to New Holland Pier had been removed, but the pier station remained and was in use as an office. Two of the LNER paddle steamers once used on the ferry service still survive. *Author*

Campbeltown was served by regular Clyde steamers until 1977. At one time railway-operated steamships served many ports and piers on the west coast of Scotland. In September 1999 the ex-LNER *Waverley*, dating from 1946 and the last sea-going paddle steamer in the world, heads 'doon the watter' to Campbeltown with an excursion. *Author*

Ryde Pier developed as the key entry to the Isle of Wight. Once with a network of about 55 miles of railway, all remaining lines were proposed for closure in the Beeching Report and surviving lines shut at the end of 1966. However, the Ryde Pier–Shanklin electrified link, together with the Isle of Wight Steam Railway's Smallbrook Junction–Wootton line, were returned to service.

The Isle of Man Steam Railway once ran boat trains to connect with passenger vessels to and from British ports. At its peak about 70 miles of narrow-gauge tramway and railway were operational. The railway routes from Douglas to Peel and Ramsey were closed in September 1968. The Douglas–Port Erin steam route, the Douglas–Ramsey electric tramway, together with the Snaefell Mountain Railway and Douglas horse trams were in use during 2017.

*Below right:* Ryde Pier is a main holiday gateway to the Isle of Wight and was a joint venture between the LSWR and LBSCR. A railway remains on the pier, but the tramway ceased in January 1969, although two short sections of tram rail can still be seen on the girders, when viewed in August 2011. Salt water does result in considerable rusting of the cast iron legs. *Author*

*Below:* Part of the LBSCR tile map at London Victoria station, seen in February 2017. It displays the network of lines that once existed on the Isle of Wight and the ferry connections from Portsmouth Harbour to both Ryde and Cowes. Osborne House is also indicated. *Author*

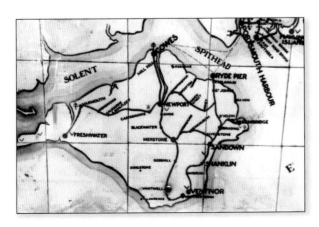

# 19
# Irish interlude

Although the island of Ireland had limited mineral wealth and population, an extensive railway network developed, to an Irish standard 5ft 3in gauge. The main line and branch line network, which peaked in the 1920s at about 3,500 miles, included narrow-gauge lines that were built mostly to serve remote rural areas. Although all were constructed to the same narrow-gauge of 3ft, they were both delightful and individualistic. At their peak there were about 500 miles of narrow-gauge passenger lines.

Some of the narrow-gauge lines were particularly innovative and the first line in the world to run on hydro-electric power was to be found at the Giant's Causeway. An inventive monorail connected Listowel with Ballybunion. Others such as the County Donegal Railways Joint Committee pioneered the use of diesel passenger railcars as far back as the 1930s and integrated these with bus services.

Although only a short sea crossing away from Britain, Irish railways are unique in their gauge, character and diversity. Yet there were links with mainland Britain in that the Belfast & Northern Counties Railway became part of the Midland Railway and was run by a managing group known as the Northern Counties Committee from 1903. The County Donegal Railways were also run by a joint committee from 1906; this also included members of the MR and the Londonderry/Derry branch became MR property.

A water tower dating from 1893, with water still in its metal tank, seen in August 2005, at Inver on the CDR Donegal–Killybegs line. Civil disorder resulted in a train being held up at Inver in 1920, whilst in 1921 the station was raided by masked gunmen. The buildings survive, although the last passenger service to stop here was on 31 December 1959. *Author*

The iconic red-liveried engines of the narrow-gauge County Donegal Railways ran on a line once partly owned by the MR of Britain. No 4 *Meenglass*, a 2-6-4T, built at Nasmyth, Wilson's Manchester Patricroft works in 1907, is pictured in the open at the Foyle Valley Railway Museum at Derry/Londonderry in August 2005. *Author*

The LNWR eventually owned the Dundalk, Newry & Greenore Railway and provided Crewe-built locomotives for the line. LNWR passenger ferries were operated from Holyhead to both Greenore and Dublin North Wall. Part of the County Donegal Railways, together with the NCC and LNWR owned lines, all became constituents of the LMS in 1923, who adopted its crimson lake livery for the NCC lines. The LMS withdrew the ferry service to Greenore in 1926 and services on this line were taken over by the GNR(I) in 1933, before closure in December 1951.

In 1922 the Irish Free State was established in the south, whilst Northern Ireland remained part of the United Kingdom. This was followed by the Irish Civil War in 1922–3, which resulted in serious damage to some railways. For example, the now closed Ballyvoyle Viaduct near Waterford was destroyed and replaced with concrete piers by Sir Robert McAlpine. In 1925 all the lines wholly within the Irish Free State were taken over by Great Southern Railways.

Nationalisation also came to the railways in Ireland. In Northern Ireland, the railways were nationalised as with those in Britain and the Ulster Transport Authority was set up in 1948. In the Republic of Ireland, nationalisation was finally achieved under the Córas Iompair Éireann in 1950. Oliver Bulleid, previously of the British Southern Railway, was taken on as Chief Mechanical Engineer for the new CIÉ. He experimented with turf-burning steam engines, but also instigated a programme of dieselisation.

Meanwhile the GNR(I), whose network of lines crossed the border between Northern Ireland and the Republic of Ireland, remained in private ownership. However, working in difficult conditions with custom checks at 14 stations, seven on each side of the border, it began to lose money. In 1953 the Great Northern Railway Board was established, effectively nationalising the railway and in 1958 the railway's rolling stock was divided up between the CIÉ and UTA.

Dublin Broadstone station was an Egyptian-styled stone building designed by J. S. Mulvany and opened in 1847. Once the hub of the Midland Great Western Railway, it was not perfectly located for the city centre and in 1937 trains were transferred to the present Connolly station, although Broadstone was still used for railway purposes until April 1961. The station is pictured in August 2005. *Author*

North Wall station at Dublin was opened by the LNWR in 1877 and regular passenger trains used the station until 1922. Two subways provided links under the road to LNWR steamers, whilst an elevated walkway once ran to the adjoining LNWR hotel. A rail freight container service used part of the ex-LNWR yard until May 2001. The station is seen in August 2005. *Author*

The North Western Hotel was opened by the LNWR at Dublin North Wall in 1884. A number of Black and Tans billeted in the hotel were attacked by the IRA in 1921. Trade never recovered and the hotel was closed by the LMS in 1923. The building became CIÉ offices and when viewed in August 2005 was used as offices for Iarnród Éireann/Irish Rail, but has since been vacated. *Author*

Many of the narrow-gauge lines had been brought into existence primarily by government funding; thus although road competition and transhipment costs brought about their decline, they were ultimately also allowed to be closed by the government. The Listowel & Ballybunion was the first closed in October 1924, mainly as a result of earlier damage during the Irish Civil War. The County Donegal Railways, the largest, ran the final passenger trains in December 1959 and the very last, the West Clare line, survived until January 1961.

On the main line network, the Westport–Achill line closed in October 1937, but most Irish gauge lines continued until nationalisation. When the UTA took over, they made extensive closures in Northern Ireland, including most cross-border ex-GNR(I) lines that gave the CIÉ no option but to close their section in the Republic. Almost all of the ex-BCDR lines, including Belfast commuter routes, were also closed by the UTA in the 1950s. The 'Derry Road' from Portadown via Omagh to Londonderry/Derry closed in February 1965 and left a huge swathe of the north without rail services. In the Republic of Ireland, the Cork–Bantry and Valentia Harbour routes were big closures, together with many remaining branch lines, in the 1960s.

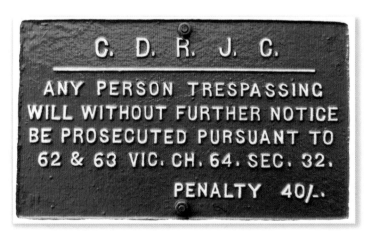

The Dublin St James's Gate Brewery had the largest urban industrial railway in Ireland. Some 8 miles of 1ft 10in narrow-gauge track linked the brewery to the main line and a quay on the River Liffey. The locomotives were designed by Samuel Geoghegan and built in Dublin. After closure in August 1975, No 23 found its way to Amberley Museum and is seen in June 1999. *Author*

The locomotives had to be restricted to horse size in the brewery, but not on the main line sidings. Ingeniously, the narrow-gauge locomotives could be lifted into a wider gauge transporter wagon. Here their wheels connected with rollers in the frame, in turn providing power for shunting on the 5ft 3in main line sidings. Such a frame is pictured at Amberley in June 1999. *Author*

The frail looking central girders of Lispole Viaduct on the Tralee & Dingle Railway are seen in August 2005. From 1929 trains were limited to 2½mph over this viaduct. Double-headed trains were required to split with Leeds-built Hunslet locomotives, weighing up to almost 40 tonnes, proceeding separately. The narrow-gauge line closed in June 1953. *Author*

The Listowel & Ballybunion Railway was the world's first working monorail, opening in 1888. It was built to the Lartigue system which had a raised central running rail. Whilst closed in October 1924, a replica of the unique locomotives used on the line was built and is pictured on a reopened section of line at Listowel in May 2005. *Author*

*Above:* The 1858 stone-built Tynan station in a derelict condition, when viewed in March 2005. It was the first station in Northern Ireland for northbound trains and custom checks were once made here. In 1950 the GNR(I) proposed closure of its entire undertaking and in October 1957 this line closed. *S. Winson*

*Left:* A closed BCDR station and small signal box at Tullymurry, in August 2003. The buildings date from 1896 and had survived for many years, since closure in January 1950. Almost all of the BCDR was closed by the UTA which was established in 1948 to take over the railways operating in Northern Ireland. *Author*

Newcastle station clock tower dates from 1903 and is seen in August 2003. The BCDR station opened in 1869 and closed in May 1955. The nearby Slieve Donard Hotel at this seaside resort was served by a siding from the station. This enabled coal to be delivered to the railway hotel's electricity plant, which in turn also lit Newcastle station. *Author*

The Valentia branch viaduct at Glensk, dating from 1893 and viewed in May 2005. The 11 spans stand up to 73ft (22m) above the river. The viaduct and other bridges on this line would have given spectacular views of Kerry. Closed in January 1960, this was once the most westerly railway in Europe. *Author*

Cahersiveen Viaduct is 940ft (286m) in length and was built in 1893 over the tidal estuary of the River Fertha. Seen in May 2005, the viaduct had been out of use since January 1960, although the guide rails for the wooden track supports gives an impression that tracks still cross the structure. *Author*

The CIÉ was the first major railway in Europe to have the majority of its services dieselised by April 1963. A Manchester-built Metro-Vick Bo-Bo C227, once used on the Valentia line and renumbered as C202, was the last survivor of its type. The diesel locomotive suffered some vandalism when seen near Valentia in May 2005 and has since been removed for eventual preservation. *Author*

More recently, the Northern Ireland Railways 'mothballed' the Lisburn–Antrim line in June 2003, but it is still used by an occasional train and there have been calls for reopening. In the Republic of Ireland, the Rosslare–Waterford line was 'suspended' for regular services in September 2010 by the current Iarnród Éireann/Irish Rail. However, under sensible new legislation the track here has to remain for at least 10 years in case there is a change of heart.

The harvesting of peat bogs has resulted in a considerable millage of narrow-gauge peat carrying railways that are still in use, but this freight network is in decline due to wider environmental concerns. On the remaining main line system, there are currently no freight services in Northern Ireland, whilst in the Republic of Ireland there are concerns about the long-term funding of a number of secondary lines.

About half of the railways opened in the island of Ireland are now closed, including all the original narrow-gauge lines. Unfortunate as this has been, it has resulted in a large number of disused lines with many fine lost viaducts and buildings still to be found years after closure. Furthermore, although a few former railway hotels have been demolished or are in new uses, most remain open. The physical legacy is enriched by some fascinating stories, poems and songs that have survived long after lines have closed such as, 'Are ye right there, Michael?' There are also a number of heritage railways and museums.

The *Titanic* sailed from Cobh in 1912 on its fateful maiden voyage. Here the *Queen Mary 2* is to be seen prior to departure for Southampton on its maiden visit to Cobh in October 2009. The railway semaphore signals in the foreground were replaced by colour-light signals shortly after. The line and ship are both still operational. *Author*

# 20
# Journeys no more

The first trains conveyed relatively few passengers and railway tickets were basically a piece of handwritten paper, torn from a book, hence the term booking office. As passenger numbers grew this stagecoach practice became increasingly unworkable.

Thomas Edmondson was a railway employee who devised a ticket-issuing process and his name became associated with railway tickets from 1838. The Edmondson ticket system provided proof of purchase, enabled accurate accountancy of the number of tickets sold, whilst the numbering system also prevented losses and fraud.

He left an enduring legacy. The card tickets were all of a standard size, they were stored in lockable wooden cabinets that enabled the different types of ticket to be easily accessed and in numerical order. He also invented a date-punch for stamping the date of issue on the tickets. The tickets could be pre-printed by the railway company concerned and tickets headed with railway initials survived right up to BR days who, at one time, printed over 300 million tickets a year.

First class tickets were often on white card, second class on pink card and third class were often green tickets, but there were exceptions with pre-Grouping companies in particular printing their tickets in other colours. To add to the mix second class was abolished by 1910, but it was not until 1956 that the remaining third class was re-designated as second class. There were special tickets for the armed services, entertainers, sports events, carers and workers. Platform tickets, return tickets that could be torn in half, child half-fare tickets, party, excursion, privilege and tickets for almost every other eventuality were offered, ranging from those for shipwrecked mariners to those for the dead in coffins.

Ballater booking office closed in February 1966 and the view here, taken in June 2009, was destroyed by fire in 2015, but is being restored. For a time at Aberdeen, the GNSR insisted tickets were purchased five minutes before the train departed and prevented entry to the platform after this time, even if connecting passengers had arrived. *Author*

*Above:* Hadlow Road was a joint station and tickets were headed L&NW and GW J'nt Rys. At one time there were through coaches to London, but the station closed to passengers in September 1956. The preserved gas lit booking office is seen in September 2000. The station now serves as a visitor centre on the Wirral Way footpath that follows much of the route of the old railway. *Author*

*Top right:* Whittingham station, on the ex-NER Alnwick–Coldstream branch, with an indication at the ticket window of which way to queue. The last ticket sold here was in September 1930, although the station remained open for freight until March 1953. This ticket window was one of two at the station to serve a small surrounding rural community and is viewed in June 2003. *Capt. J. Roddis*

*Middle:* Overstrand ticket window was situated on the island platform, which was accessed by a subway. Seen in July 2008, the station remains largely intact, although closed in April 1953. Tickets were also available on the train if the ticket office was closed. This is one of just two remaining former NSJ stations. *Author*

*Right:* A rather austere ticket window in a brick wall at Potton station on the Oxford–Cambridge line, seen in September 1994. The building dates from 1862 and served the last tickets in January 1968. After closure, the building was saved from demolition by a former railway employee and still survives. *Author's collection*

The Railway Clearing House, near Euston, opened in 1842 after the Edmondson tickets were generally adopted by all railways. The organisation was set up to manage, audit and facilitate fair receipts for through workings between the various railway companies. The Railway Clearing House continued with railway activities until 1963 and its huge Eversholt Street office building remains.

The first season tickets were issued on the Canterbury & Whitstable Railway in 1834 mainly for Canterbury passengers wishing to visit the seaside at Whitstable. Season tickets eventually became widespread for workers, often from the new suburbs created by the railways, ranging from weekly to longer periods. Many were originally in the form of small embossed leather booklets, but metal tokens were issued for the entire working life of quarrymen using the Dinorwic quarry workmen's trains.

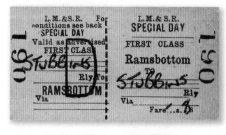

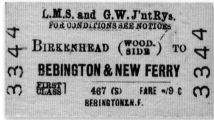

Tickets issued at stations were nearly always obtained from the booking office. Although each railway had different designs for booking offices, the overall concept was the same. A small opening allowed tickets to be exchanged for money without compromising security. Some railways had 'In' and 'Out' notices to ensure order, whilst others had strict opening times to try and prevent any last-minute rush. The stock of tickets provided at many stations was considerable and some pre-Grouping tickets to little used destinations survived until automation in the late 1980s.

Wolferton station was the closest to Sandringham House. Special arrangements were made for royalty and at one time tickets bearing 'H.M. the King', and with the destination Sandringham, would have been kept by an equerry. A platform entry box is viewed here in August 1994. Closed in May 1969, the last Royal Train used the station in 1966. *Author*

The Aldwych branch distinctive booking office windows, seen in September 1997, were also to be found at other Piccadilly line stations. The first electric ticket issuing machines were provided at London Underground stations and today ticket windows have been replaced by ticket machines. *Author*

Tickets were also sold on the trains when unstaffed halts were provided. In later years, after more and more stations became unstaffed, this led to conductor-guards on trains, not only clipping tickets with nippers, but also carrying a rack of tickets. These were similar to those used on a bus or tram, with which the auto-trains in particular were designed to compete. In later years portable ticket machines that issued paper bus type tickets on the train became commonplace. Yet, until the arrival of ticket computerisation, the various excess fare tickets issued on trains were still on paper forms filled in by hand and torn from a book.

A mechanised ticket machine was installed at Birmingham Snow Hill in 1911. Rapid printer machines were also used on London Underground in the early 1900s, but it was not until 1990 that Edmondson tickets were finally replaced by larger, magnetically coded card tickets on the main line railways.

Not all tickets were collected after use; many were saved or bought by railway enthusiasts, particularly where closure was imminent. Survival has been rather random, but scarcity broadly dictates current value. The variety of different tickets illustrated in this chapter were collected by your author on his travels and are all to and from stations that are closed. They represent journeys that can no longer be made by train and are tangible evidence of lost lines and services.

Services from Smethwick West ended in September 1996 when a new interchange station was opened nearby. The smashed-up booking office is seen in August 2001. This is most likely to be mindless vandalism, but robberies were occasionally carried out as large sums of cash could once be kept at ticket offices, particularly when annual season tickets were renewed. *Author*

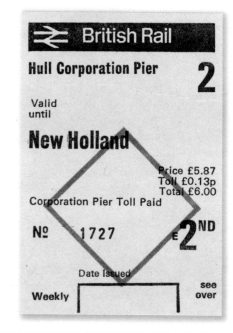

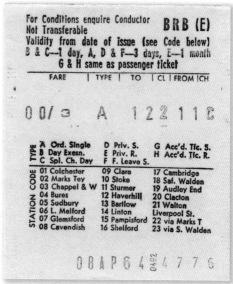

# 21
# Branch line time line

A relatively dense network of secondary and branch lines developed and by 1900 covered most populated parts of the country. The branches included an eclectic mix of stations, but on occasions these incorporated some of the most distinguished buildings in the area that they served. Many were well maintained with gardens and a range of facilities for passengers and freight.

Some distinctive stations stem from the early railway companies. Local building materials and contractors were generally used and there was a myriad of early designs, even on relatively short branches. The closed Newtyle station in Scotland and Hampton in the Midlands, both dating from the 1830s, are two of the earliest branch line stations still existing, but could not be more different in design.

A number of stations that were built proved to be larger than the traffic warranted, such as Oswestry, Llanidloes and Crieff. Others proved too small and had to be replaced, such as at Fleetwood and Alnwick. A number of stations were badly located for the area they served such as Thaxted, whilst the word 'Road' was added to indicate that the station was some way from the settlement named, such as Maentwrog Road being two miles from Maentwrog. Others were located in the very heart of settlements, from Ballater to Bude.

Cirencester. May 1841–April 1964, almost 123 years in use. Cirencester Town station, which became part of the GWR, included a most unusual Gothic stone tower, reputedly designed by I. K. Brunel. It is pictured in June 1993 and still survives. Cirencester, once served by two stations, today has none, but returning trains to the town has been considered. *Author*

Richmond. October 1846–March 1969, 122 years 6 months in use. The station was designed by George Andrews and completed in an attractive style to blend in with the Yorkshire town. The branch was well used, including by military staff to nearby Catterick Military Camp. Freight was withdrawn in 1967 and passenger services deliberately run down. The station is seen in July 1996 and still survives. *Author*

Alnwick. August 1850–October 1968, 118 years 2 months in use. The substantially built terminus designed by William Bell for the NER replaced an earlier station in 1887. The later terminus reflected Alnwick Castle in its solid stone construction. Passenger services ceased in January 1968. Progress is being made in reopening the branch by the heritage Aln Valley Railway, but the station, seen in October 1996, is unlikely to be reused. *Author*

On some branches a pride was taken in never designing two stations alike. However, several railway companies went on to develop more recognisable station styles of their own. Introduced by Brunel on the GWR, economies were sometimes made by railway companies through the standardisation of station designs. Nevertheless, even if a number of passenger stations became somewhat similar in design, the materials used to build them often varied. On the other hand, station furniture, paint colour, uniforms and ambiance were usually all unmistakably of a corporate nature.

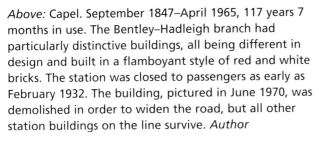

*Above:* Capel. September 1847–April 1965, 117 years 7 months in use. The Bentley–Hadleigh branch had particularly distinctive buildings, all being different in design and built in a flamboyant style of red and white bricks. The station was closed to passengers as early as February 1932. The building, pictured in June 1970, was demolished in order to widen the road, but all other station buildings on the line survive. *Author*

*Above right:* Maldon East. October 1848–April 1966, 117 years 6 months in use. The impressive Jacobean building with a colonial-style frontage is seen in August 1994. The public face of the railway could sometimes lead to ornate buildings, even on branch lines. Here at Maldon, a suitably grand station was built with the aid of the local MP. Passenger closure came in September 1964. *Author*

*Middle:* Alton Towers. July 1849–January 1965, 115 years 6 months in use. The Italianate villa-influenced station is pictured in September 1993. Used by the Earl of Shrewsbury, a lift was installed for luggage to reach the road above. Although on a secondary route, the NSR station could once accommodate 12-coach trains. 'Towers' was added to the name in 1954 and freight ceased in June 1964. *Author*

*Right* Oswestry. May 1860–December 1971, 111 years 7 months in use. The Italianate-styled building was designed by Benjamin Piercy. Once the headquarters of the Cambrian Railways, an imposing image, partly viewed in October 2002, was considered important. The station closed to passengers in November 1966, but freight continued to use the line through the station until 1988. Cambrian Heritage Railways aim to reopen the branch to Gobowen. *Author*

Aboyne. December 1859–July 1966, 106 years 7 months in use. The station, built in granite for the GNSR, is seen in June 2009. It was used by Queen Victoria on her trips to Balmoral, before the line was extended to Ballater. A camping coach was also once provided at the station. Passenger services on the route, which in many ways was a long branch line, ceased in February 1966. *Author*

Wolferton. October 1862–May 1969, 106 years 7 months in use. The view, seen in August 1994, is of the Tudor-styled replacement station that opened in 1898. Ornate private royal retiring rooms allowed easy access to horse-drawn carriages. No expense was spared by the GER for the monarch's interchange to nearby Sandringham House. The line was eventually reduced in status to an unstaffed branch. *Author*

Petworth. October 1859–May 1966, 106 years 7 months in use. Passenger services ended in February 1955. The station was located almost two miles from the town and the current ex-LBSCR building dates from 1892. The station is seen in April 1995. The wooden building is now a hotel run in conjunction with a number of Pullman coaches on the site. *Author*

Cromdale. July 1863–November 1968, 105 years 4 months in use. The station looks a little like a traditional stone Scottish croft dwelling and has been restored to original GNSR appearance. It is seen in October 2011. Passenger services ended in October 1965, although a freight line once ran from the station to the nearby whisky distillery at Balmenach, also closing in 1968. *Author*

Framlingham. June 1859–April 1963, 103 years 10 months in use. The terminus of the branch from Wickham Market Junction, on the East Suffolk Line, is seen in June 2012. The branch closed to passengers in November 1952, but between 1954–8 special through coaches from and to London were run at the beginning and end of term for students at Framlingham College. *Author*

Holbeach. November 1858–May 1965, 106 years 6 months in use. Passenger services ended in February 1959 and the station is seen in November 2009. The M&GN was downgraded to a secondary route by the LNER. In 2015, after some neglect, the building was used for residential accommodation. *Author*

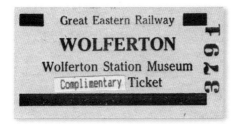

Llanidloes. August 1864–December 1967, 103 years 4 months in use. The Georgian-styled building, designed by Benjamin Piercy, was once the headquarters of the Mid-Wales Railway. The station was rather large for the sparse population it served. Plans to demolish the structure for a road scheme were thwarted and it remained in September 2003. Passenger services ended in December 1962. *Author*

Gedney. July 1862–May 1965, 102 years 10 months in use. Passenger services were withdrawn in February 1959. The station was rather unusual in design. It was entirely different to nearby Holbeach, even though the same railway was originally extended eastward towards Sutton Bridge. Located some way from the village it served, it is seen here an ever-derelict condition in November 2009, but there are plans to use the building as an office. *Author*

Coalport. February 1862–November 1963, 101 years 9 months in use. The station was called Coalport West by BR, but was closed to passengers in September 1963. The station is seen in September 1993. In 2017 carriages at the station were used for holiday accommodation, whilst the line south of Bridgenorth has been reopened by the heritage Severn Valley Railway. *Author*

Bovey. July 1866–December 1967, 101 years 5 months in use. The stone-built station remained in good condition when photographed in September 1993. Passenger services ended in March 1959, but freight trains continued to pass through the station until July 1970. Subsequently part of the branch line here has been replaced by a road. *Author*

Chard Central. September 1866–October 1966, 100 years 1 month in use. The attractive station, which became part of the GWR and once contained broad gauge track, still has an overall roof. 'Central' was added to the name in 1949, although it was not that centrally located to the town. Passenger services ceased in February 1964 and it is seen in September 1993. *Author*

BR did not always respect the wonderful architectural inheritance of the railways. Many stations were stripped of their platform canopies, unsympathetic changes were made, and there were part demolitions, mutilations, or hideous extensions. This ruined the integrity of some of the original buildings, but was better than complete demolition.

Although residential railway property has mostly survived, large numbers of disused and underused station

Ballater. October 1866–July 1966, 99 years 9 months in use. Passenger services ended in February 1966. The GNSR-built station was provided with royal facilities approved by Queen Victoria. The terminus was used by royalty and dignitaries from around the world. Viewed in June 2009, the original wooden buildings were destroyed by fire in 2015, but are being replaced. *Author*

Llanerchymedd. February 1866–December 1964, 98 years 10 months in use. Freight continued to use the branch past the station until 1993. The station became part of the LNWR and is seen from a steam-hauled train in July 1964. Situated on the Isle of Anglesey, the branch track remains heavily overgrown, but the platform buildings are used as a heritage centre and café. *Author*

buildings were demolished by BR. This was the cheapest option, often simply to deter vandalism, without any serious thought to the attractiveness, or any subsequent use of the buildings. In some cases the sites simply remained vacant or derelict for many years. As a consequence, many branch stations have been lost. Examples from well-known settlements that no longer have original station buildings include Brecon, Buckingham, Haverhill, Tadcaster, Thame and Wetherby. Numerous demolitions were due to the buildings being in a state of disrepair before closure. BR and, for that matter, the Big Four before, just did not have the cash available for proper maintenance of everything and the long-term neglect of many buildings ensued.

BR also demolished some attractive buildings subversively and quickly to foil attempts to save them. As a consequence, a number of railway buildings became 'listed buildings' which gave greater protected status. Despite this safeguard, the beautiful listed classical old station at Newmarket was demolished. Other attractive station buildings have been sold off, even where lines remain open and await the varying decisions of their new owners. Even today the threat of demolition is ever present; Trimley station has been deliberately neglected by Network Rail, as has the last remaining 19th century operational wooden footbridge in Britain and arguably in the world at Alton station.

Luckily, after an endless list of railway closures, with damage and demolition to stations, many closed railway stations of great distinction can still be found throughout the country. Hidden treasures, surviving on closed branches and secondary routes, can be found throughout Britain. Surviving closed station buildings can be found in range of architectural styles. For example, a classical Ashby-de-la-Zouch, an Italianate Alton Towers, a Gothic almost monastic-styled Richmond, a Tudor Stamford East, a Jacobean Maldon East, a Georgian Llanidloes, a baronial Aboyne and a functional Brunel-designed terminus at Ashburton.

Stoke Golding. August 1873–July 1971, about 98 years of line use. The LNWR & MR jointly-owned station was at the start of a branch to Hinckley, but this was decommissioned in 1888, without ever being used. The station was closed to passengers by the LMS in April 1931 and to local freight in August 1962. The line was finally used for the storage of wagons. Part of the station is observed in August 2008. *Author*

Wretham & Hockham. January 1869–June 1964, 95 years 5 months in use. Located on the Thetford–Swaffham line in Norfolk, the GER-built station is pictured in September 1994. Built from knapped (split) flints, a number of other Norfolk stations were also built in this local material. *Author*

Cambus O'May. Spring 1876–February 1966, about 90 years in use. The wooden station was built for the GNSR and was open by March 1876. The Deeside Way footpath now uses the former trackbed which is seen in June 2009. A ferry crossed the River Dee here, until it was replaced by a pedestrian suspension bridge in 1905. The bridge was damaged by floods in 2015. *Author*

Ashburton. May 1872–September 1962, 90 years 4 months in use. The station, soon to become part of the GWR, was the terminus of the branch from Totnes and the interior is seen here in September 1993. After closure, the heritage Dart Valley Railway used the station for a short period 1969–71. Planning proposals that would have blocked the railway returning to the station were withdrawn in 2017. *Author*

Hawes. October 1878–April 1964, 85 years 6 months in use. The station lost its ex-NER passenger service to Northallerton in April 1954 and the ex-MR infrequent passenger service to Hawes Junction, now Garsdale, in March 1959. There are plans to extend the heritage Wensleydale Railway to this station, which is used as part of the Dales Museum. The picture was taken in September 1993. *Author*

Reepham. May 1881–May 1964, 83 years in use. The rather plain yellow brick GER-built Norfolk station closed to passengers in September 1952. After closure to freight, the line through the station was still used to serve a concrete works at Lenwade until July 1981. The building, seen in September 1994, is currently used as a café. *Author*

Bottisham & Lode. June 1884–July 1964, 80 years 1 month in use. The station is seen in a derelict state in March 2012. The design of the station was similar to that at Mildenhall. Although only one freight train a day used the branch after passenger closure in June 1962, the signal box remained manned until complete closure. *Author's collection*

Pontfadog. 1873–July 1935, about 62 years in use. This waiting room, restored and seen in June 1999, on the route of the narrow-gauge Glyn Valley Tramway in Wales, was provided two years after the passenger services had commenced in 1891. An open fire and seats still could not compete with the bus and passenger services ceased in April 1933. *Author*

Strathpeffer. June 1885–March 1951, 65 years 9 months in use. Passenger services to the station ended in February 1946. The largely wooden HR-built terminus was once served by the 'Strathpeffer Spa Express'. A narrow-gauge tourist railway may in the future use part of the branch and serve the station, seen in June 2010. *Author*

St Laurence. July 1897–September 1952, 55 years 2 months in use. St Laurence, on the ex-Isle of Wight Central Railway, was provided on the second route that once ran to Ventnor and was located on a scenic part of the line. The station was downgraded to an unstaffed halt by the SR in 1927. The view was taken in August 1986. *Author*

Stations still standing in every type of building material also survive; for example, Hawes in stone, Swaffham in flint, Pocklington in brick, Petworth in wood and Camber in corrugated iron. Some combined other materials such as tiles and rendering to provide endless varieties of building, whilst a good selection of rural stations can additionally be found on Britain's heritage railways.

A number of closed stations also survive on the coast and several have been used for residential accommodation such as at Padstow, Lynton, Hornsea, St Lawrence and Yarmouth on the Isle of Wight, Wells-next-the-Sea, Overstrand, Cloughton, Robin Hood's Bay and Kettleness. Lightly built coastal railway stations at Camber, Portsoy and Lybster have all been used as club houses.

It is fascinating to consider that when an isolated remain is to be found, it was formerly part of a bustling branch line, once with busy passenger and freight workings. Even at many branch stations there may well have been at one time a station master, porters, booking office staff, goods staff and signalmen, often in sufficient numbers at most grades to cover for two shifts. In a relatively short time in the 1960s many of these railway employees were swept away. Finally, by taking the opening and closing dates for all the illustrated stations in this chapter, it is clear that lost branch lines had an average life time of about 90 years.

Overstrand. August 1906–April 1953, 46 years 8 months in use. The building is one of just two ex-NSJ stations still surviving. The island platform was accessed via a subway. The station was used on occasion by Winston Churchill, whose family holidayed at the quiet Norfolk seaside resort. The station is seen in July 2008. *Author*

Camber Golf Links. July 1895–September 1939, 44 years 2 months in use. On the Rye & Camber narrow-gauge railway, the station became an unstaffed halt in 1935. The line was requisitioned by the government during World War 2, but ended up in such a run-down condition it never reopened. The corrugated iron built station remained after closure and is seen here in September 1999. *Author*

Yarde Halt. July 1925–March 1965, 39 years 8 months in use. On the line south of Torrington, the small halt was opened by the SR to serve nearby clay workings and milk trains that were attached to passenger services. Freight continued to use the line past the halt until August 1982 and track was removed in 1984. The remote halt is seen in August 1995 and is now on the Tarka Trail. *Author*

Blackmoor. May 1898–September 1935, 37 years 4 months in use. Situated on the narrow-gauge Lynton & Barnstaple Railway, the stone base of the former water tower and overgrown pipes are seen in September 1995. The distinctive main station building also remains at Blackmoor and is currently used as a restaurant.
*Author*

Roundwood Halt. August 1927–June 1947, 19 years 10 months in use. The tiny halt on the Harpenden–Hemel Hempstead branch was opened by the LMS to cater for new housing development. It was closed as a temporary measure due to a coal shortage, but the line never reopened to passengers. Remaining freight running past the halt to the Hemelite Concrete Company ceased in July 1979. The view here is in February 1981.
*Author*

# 22
# Ten Great British lost scenic railway journeys

As the railway network spread across the face of Britain it did much to change the countryside. Although it is clear that in many locations care was taken to try and mitigate the damage to the landscape, more often care was taken not to upset the view of the local lord of the manor and landowner. Nevertheless, huge earthworks and viaducts made scars on the countryside, but they gradually began to be absorbed into the landscape and today, with mature trees being allowed to grow on railway property, they have become an integral and much loved part of the landscape. The railway also invariably added a further dimension to the landscape, the continuity of the railway line contrasting with the patchwork of fields.

There are numerous lost lines that served beautiful areas; many picturesque scenes from the window of these lost lines would have been stunning. I note from my diary that I was impressed by the scenery on lines to Ballachulish, Padstow, Woodhead, Bacup, Richmond (Yorks), Bridport and Brightlingsea. I know there are of course very many more that could be added to the list and that readers will have their own favourites, but in selecting just 10 lost scenic lines, in no specific order, I have simply included my own preferences and those praised in Bradshaw's Guide. I have focused on 10 lines in the countryside. However, I could not resist just including one additional line, the Liverpool Overhead Railway, simply for what once must have been its spectacular overhead views of docklands and industry.

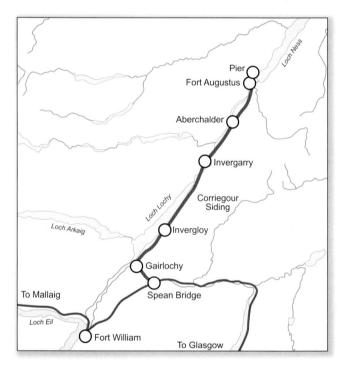

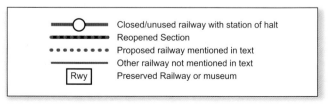

Key to maps

○ Closed/unused railway with station of halt
Reopened Section
Proposed railway mentioned in text
Other railway not mentioned in text
Rwy Preserved Railway or museum

The remote Spean Bridge–Fort Augustus branch ran along the Great Glen, which Bradshaw described as being 'naturally filled with water and formed of a long chain of lakes'. The Pier station on Loch Ness at Fort Augustus was the first station on the line to close to passengers in September 1906 and freight in July 1924; remains are seen in June 2010. *Author*

| FORT-AUGUSTUS and SPEAN BRIDGE.—Invergarry and Fort-Augustus.—North British. | | | | | | | | | | | | |
|---|---|---|---|---|---|---|---|---|---|---|---|---|
| Mls | | mrn | aft | aft | | Mls | | mrn | aft | aft | | |
| 1 | Fort-Augustus....dep. | 8 30 | 2 30 | 7 15 | | 2¾ | Spean Bridge ....dep. | 1025 | 4 10 | 9 15 | | |
| 4½ | Aberchalder............ | 8 39 | 2 42 | 7 27 | | 7½ | Gairlochy ............ | 1033 | 4 22 | 9 27 | | |
| 9 | Invergarry ............ | 8 51 | 2 56 | 7 41 | | 15 | Invergloy Platform... | Sig. | Sig. | Sig. | | |
| 16½ | Invergloy Platform.... | Sig. | Sig. | Sig. | | 19½ | Invergarry ............ | 1059 | 4 59 | 10 4 | | |
| 21½ | Gairlochy ............ | 9 17 | 3 33 | 8 18 | | 23 | Aberchalder............ | 1111 | 5 13 | 1018 | | |
| 24 | Spean Bridge /above/ | 9 25 | 3 45 | 8 30 | | 24 | Fort-Augustus....arr. | 1120 | 5 25 | 1030 | | |

Fort Augustus–Spean Bridge timetable April 1910.

## The Great Glen to Loch Ness

The 24-mile Spean Bridge–Fort Augustus route was built north of Ben Nevis along the Great Glen in Scotland and onto the shores of Loch Ness. Opening in 1903, the railway was constructed to main line standards as a possible route to Inverness. This was never achieved and, running in such a remote area, services were first withdrawn in October 1911.

This early railway closure met with a storm of local protest, together with national concern as the line had been open for just seven years. As a consequence, services over the route were reinstated by the NBR in August 1913. Nevertheless, only a handful of passengers a day used the line and the remaining section finally closed to passengers in December 1933. After this, just one coal train a week ran until December 1946.

The views from this line would have been of splendid remote Scottish Highland countryside. The natural beauty would have been enhanced by a chain of lochs, rivers, forests and mountains along the route, before the line crossed the Caledonian Canal and River Oich to arrive on the shores of Loch Ness. Part of the trackbed is now used by the Great Glen Way and a museum is to be found at Invergarry station.

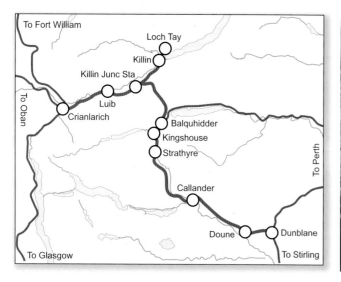

The abandoned trackbed beyond Killin to the station at Loch Tay, pictured in September 1983, with the bridge over the River Lochay in view. LMS steamers from Loch Tay ceased operating to Kenmore Pier in September 1939. The Killin–Loch Tay section closed to passenger traffic at the same time, although it remained in use to stable the branch locomotive until September 1965. *Author*

## Crossing the Trossachs

The 40-mile Dunblane–Crianlarich line opened in 1880. The route not only served the towns of Doune and Callander, but also Balquhidder; the latter had romantic connections with Rob Roy. Yet the ex-CR line was simply seen as duplicating an entirely different route to Crianlarich and was closed in September 1965 as a result of a rock fall, but then officially in November 1965, as a result of the Beeching Report.

I was fortunate enough to travel on this route in a dining car in 1965. It was a spectacularly attractive mountain line running through part of the wild, tangled and beautiful Trossachs, through the Pass of Leny, along the shores of Loch Lubnaig and over Glen Ogle Viaduct. It climbed through an area known as the 'Khyber Pass' of Scotland, to reach the remote and more wooded Killin Junction where a connection could once be made to the shores of Loch Tay, where in turn a steamer service operated. The main line then ran from Killin Junction, along the beautiful Glen Dochart and past Ben More to Crianlarich. Parts of the trackbed are now used by the Rob Roy Way and parts by the A85 road.

Bradshaw reported that Callander on the Dunblane–Crianlarich line was 'the centre of a most beautiful and highly picturesque district'. The mountain scenery that could have been observed from the train is seen in October 2011, near the viaduct at Glen Ogle. The trackbed is now used as a footpath. *Capt. J. Roddis*

| BARNSTAPLE TOWN and LYNTON.—Lynton and Barnstaple. | | | | | | | | | | | | | | | | | | | | |
|---|---|---|---|---|---|---|---|---|---|---|---|---|---|---|---|---|---|---|---|---|
| Sec. and Man., Charles E. Drewett, Pilton Bridge, Barnstaple. | | | | | | | | | | | | | | | | | | | | |
| **Down.** | | Week Days. | | | | | Sundays. | | **Up.** | | | Week Days. | | | | | | Sundays. | | |
| Miles. | | mrn | mrn | mrn | aft | aft | | mrn | Miles. | | mrn | mrn | aft | aft | aft | | | aft | | |
| — | Barnstaple Town ¶...dep. | 6 20 | 9 5 | 10 30 | 4 40 | 5 35 | | 7 30 | — | Lynton...........dep. | 8 20 | 10 45 | 12 20 | 6 30 | 7 10 | | | 5 38 | | |
| 5 | Chelfham ¶............... | 6 40 | 9 25 | 10 56 | 5 15 | 5 54 | | 7 50 | 3½ | Woody Bay ¶........... | 8 35 | 11 1 | 12 36 | 6 46 | 7 25 | | | 5 54 | | |
| 8 | Bratton Fleming...... | 6 57 | 9 42 | 11 5 | 5 17 | 6 9 | | 8 5 | 7½ | Blackmoor ¶............ | 8 53 | 11 22 | 12 54 | 7 5 | 7 43 | | | 6 12 | | |
| 12 | Blackmoor ¶............ | 7 18 | 10 0 | 11 23 | 5 35 | 6 27 | | 8 23 | 11½ | Bratton Fleming...... | 9 10 | 11 39 | 1 12 | 7 23 | 8 0 | | | 6 29 | | |
| 16 | Woody Bay ¶.......... | 7 38 | 10 19 | 11 42 | 5 55 | 6 47 | | 8 42 | 14½ | Chelfham ............[49 | 9 24 | 11 53 | 1 27 | 7 39 | 8 15 | | | 6 44 | | |
| 19½ | Lynton ‖...........arr. | 7 53 | 10 34 | 11 57 | 6 10 | 7 2 | | 8 57 | 19½ | Barnstaple Town ††arr. | 9 42 | 12 11 | 1 46 | 7 57 | 8 34 | | | 7 3 | | |

†† Over ¾ mile to Barnstaple (G. W.).          ‖ Station for Lynmouth.
¶ "Halts" at Snapper (for Goodleigh), between Barnstaple Town and Chelfham, but during daylight only ; and at Parracombe, between Blackmoor and Woody Bay.

Lynton & Barnstaple timetable April 1910.

The route from Barnstaple Town following the River Yeo, crossed Chelfham Viaduct whilst climbing scenic and steep-sided valleys to Bratton Fleming. It then skirted Parracombe and Woody Bay, where the line reached a summit that was the highest part of the SR. The railway eventually arrived at the cliff-top terminus at the coastal town of Lynton, which in turn still has a funicular link to Lynmouth below. A section of this distinctive and lovely scenic railway, in the Exmoor National Park, has been reopened at Woody Bay by the Lynton & Barnstaple heritage railway and more of this sleeping beauty will follow.

## Perchance it is not dead, but sleepeth

The 19½-mile, 1ft 11½in narrow-gauge Lynton & Barnstaple Railway ran from its terminus at Barnstaple Town to Lynton on the North Devon coast. The railway opened in 1898. The rugged terrain encountered, crossing the shoulder of Exmoor, resulted in construction costs being twice what had been anticipated. This bankrupted the contractor, but provided a delightfully scenic railway. Uniquely for an English narrow-gauge line, the route was heavily engineered; the railway included the eight-span Chelfham Viaduct and the now destroyed Lancey Brook Viaduct, together with about 80 other bridges. Winter traffic was disappointing, but closure came with real sadness in September 1935.

The L&B ran through Exmoor that Bradshaw described as 'wild and beautiful-magnificent and lovely'. On the winding route between Barnstaple and Lynton, the summit of the line at almost 1,000ft (305m) was the highest point on the SR. The tall viaduct at Chelfham, seen in September 1995, provided views of a tributary to the River Yeo below. *Author*

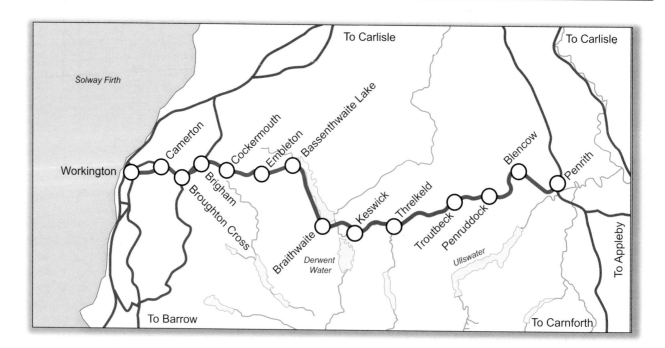

## Across the Northern Lakes

The 31-mile Cockermouth, Keswick & Penrith Railway ran from Penrith to Cockermouth and was then was continued by the LNWR to the coast at Workington. The line cut an east-west route through the northern part of the Lake District, opening for all traffic by 1865. It served the key centre of Keswick, where a hotel was directly connected to the station. Traffic was buoyant and single-line sections were doubled by 1900. DMUs were introduced in 1955; they had the advantage of allowing fine views from their front and rear windows, but were unable to save the line. The line west of Keswick closed in April 1966. The remaining route was designated in 1967 as part of the Network for Development, but after a fight and upset, closed in March 1972, with freight surviving on a short section for a few months more.

I travelled on this line when snow could still be seen on Skiddaw. The route showed off some spectacular views of the northern fells, lakes and forests in this part of the Lake District. The railway followed the River Greta to Keswick, after that it continued westward via the beautiful shores of Bassenthwaite Lake and the Derwent Valley to Cockermouth. Part of the line west of Keswick has been used by the A66, but there are hopes of reopening the Keswick–Penrith section.

A glimpse towards the Lakes from the ex-Whitehaven, Cleator & Egremont Joint Railway in July 2009. Bradshaw enthuses about the 'lofty mountains, naked hills, bleak barren moors and grassy well wooded fells' of the area. The line seen here in July 2009, joined the Keswick route at Marron Junction, was last used for regular freight in May 1954 and abandoned in 1960. *Author*

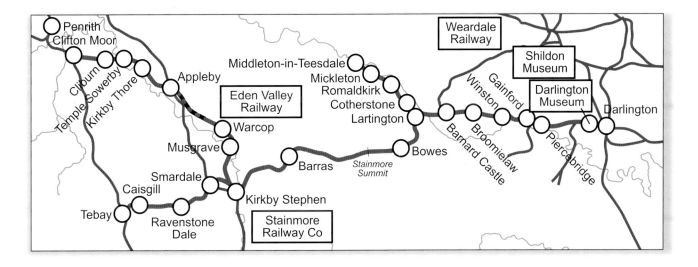

# Over the roof of England

The 64¾-mile NER trans-Pennine Darlington–Penrith route, together with the 11¾-mile link to Tebay, was built with the intention of conveying coal and coke from Durham to the iron works of Cumbria. It was built in stages over Stainmore, opening throughout in 1862. The line involved severe gradients and substantial engineering works in running over the bleak Pennines. The area was regularly affected by snow and fog, in particular near the Stainmore Summit, where the railway could sometimes be closed for days during the winter.

Inevitable decline set in and the line closed in stages, ending its trans-Pennine role. The remaining section closed to passenger traffic in November 1964 and to freight in March of the following year. After closure an act of destruction saw the demolition of the great wrought and cast iron viaduct at Belah, the second highest in the country.

The views from parts of this railway would be spectacular, particularly where it used the Stainmore Gap, between the Upper Tees and the Upper Eden valleys, the highest, bleakest and most difficult of all the Pennine gap routes. The sweeping, treeless moorland landscapes on the highest parts of the line would have been delightful. One of the highlights would have been crossing the high Belah Viaduct, together with those over the River Tees and at Deepdale. A branch off this line to Middleton-in-Teesdale has been turned into the Tees Valley Railway Path, while the Stainmore Railway Company and Eden Valley Railway operate over parts of the line.

The trackbed at Stainmore approaching the summit from the east in November 2013. At 1,370ft (418m), Stainmore was the highest summit on any English main line railway route. Bradshaw rightly describes the Pennine area as being 'bleak and barren'.
*Copyright Trevor Littlewood: Creative Common Licence*

Another route over the Pennines was from Northallerton via Wensleydale and Hawes to Garsdale. The station at Hawes was served towards the end with just one passenger train a day, until March 1959. Hawes is 774ft (236m) above sea level and the line is seen here in September 1993. The heritage Wensleydale Railway operates over the eastern part of this route. *Author*

Darlington–Penrith timetable September 1955.

**NORTH EASTERN RAILWAY.**

From YORK.

**PIERCE BRIDGE**

*N. E. R.*

**BARRAS.**

## Climbing into the Brecon Beacons

The Brecon & Merthyr Railway reached Brecon from Talybont in 1863 and was extended to Merthyr Tydfil in 1868 with the help of the LNWR. The 24¼-mile northern section of the railway between Brecon and Merthyr had been a difficult line to construct, crossing a remote area of the Brecon Beacons. The highest tunnel above sea level in Britain was on this line at Torpantau. The tunnel was reached from Merthyr by a gruelling seven miles of 1 in 38 climb. The Pontsticill Junction–Merthyr section closed to passengers in November 1961. The Brecon–Talyllyn Junction–Pontsticill Junction section closed to passengers in December 1962 and to goods in May 1964, ending all rail services to Brecon.

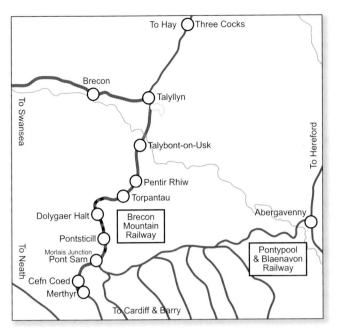

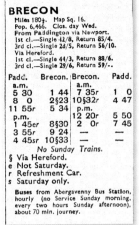

**BRECON**
Miles 180½.  Map Sq. 16.
Pop. 6,466.  Clos. day Wed.
From Paddington via Newport.
1st cl.—Single 42/8, Return 85/4.
3rd cl.—Single 28/5, Return 56/10.
Via Hereford.
1st cl.—Single 44/3, Return 88/6.
3rd cl.—Single 29/6, Return 59/-.

| Padd. | Brecon. | Brecon. | Padd. |
|-------|---------|---------|-------|
| a.m. | | a.m. | |
| 5 30 | 1 44 | 7 35r | 1 0 |
| 8 0 | 2§23 | 10§32r | 4 47 |
| 11 55r | 5 34 | p.m. | |
| p.m. | | 12 20r | 5 50 |
| 1 45er | 8§30 | 2 0r | 7 45 |
| 3 55r | 9 24 | — | — |
| 4 45sr | 10§33 | — | — |

*No Sunday Trains.*
§ Via Hereford.
e Not Saturday.
r Refreshment Car.
s Saturday only.

**Buses** from Abergavenny Bus Station, hourly (no Service Sunday morning, every two hours Sunday afternoon), about 70 min. journey.

Brecon departures April 1956.

A bridge approaching Pontsarn Viaduct on the ex-BM & LNWR Joint Railway. Bradshaw described Brecon as 'situated in the midst of very beautiful mountain scenery'. The viaduct walls seen ahead rose to 92ft (28m) over the Taf Fechan. The trackbed is now part of the Taff Trail cycleway and footpath. The view was taken in September 2003. *Author*

Another route to Brecon, with the Brecon Beacons looming in the background, was the ex-Neath & Brecon line from Colbren Junction. Passenger services ended in October 1962. Freight remained on a southern section of line to a quarry adjacent to Penwyllt station until 1977 and this site is seen in September 2003. *Author*

The line was picturesque, traversing a high curving viaduct at Cefn Coed, giving views of Merthyr Tydfil and coal mining areas. It then climbed through woodland into the wilder and eventually bleak countryside of the Brecon Beacons, crossing Pontsarn Viaduct, as well as passing through tunnels to reach Brecon. A part is now used by the Taff Trail, a cycleway and footpath, whilst the Brecon Mountain Railway, a narrow-gauge line opened in 1980, uses the Pant–Torpantau section.

## Snowdonia lake and slate

The 24¾-mile Bala–Blaenau Ffestiniog line was heavily engineered and was completed in 1883, primarily to reach the lucrative slate producing area at Blaenau Ffestiniog. There were two viaducts on the route and the largest, the nine-arched Cwm Prysor, towered over the Afon Prysor.

The line, which became part of the GWR, served a very remote area, but at one time slate workers used the railway and halts were provided for local farms. The line closed to regular passenger trains in January 1960, but the short Bala–Bala Junction section survived until January 1965.

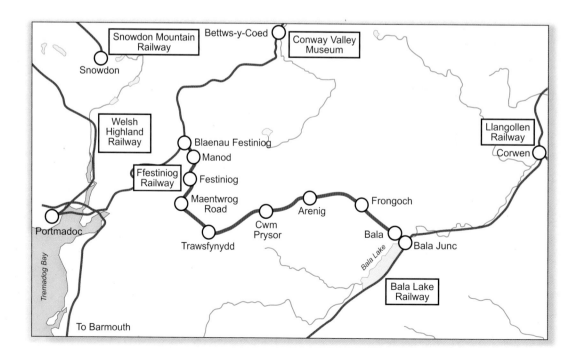

North Wales, with the disused ex-LNWR line between Bala and Blaenau Ffestiniog in view. It is apparent when this photograph was taken in September 2003 that the views from the train near Cwm Prysor, cut high into the mountainside in the Snowdonia National Park, on a clear day would have been spectacular. *Author*

Located in the Snowdonia area of North Wales, north of Bala, spectacular bleak and rugged mountain views would have been seen as the line climbed and twisted towards Blaenau Ffestiniog. This included running on a remote ledge high in the mountains, where nesting birds of prey are still to be found. Arriving at Blaenau Ffestiniog, the varied but mostly green mountain scenery would change to the grey wastes left by the huge slate workings. A Ffestiniog–Trawsfynydd freight link to serve a nuclear power station survived until October 1998 and overgrown track on this section is looked upon for a possible heritage railway revival.

## The Wye Valley

The 14¾-mile GWR Monmouth–Chepstow line included two tunnels, together with three bridges over the River Wye, opening in 1876. While serving the popular attraction of Tintern Abbey, the rural line closed to passengers in January 1959 and to all traffic in January 1964, although a short southern section remained to Tintern Quarry until March 1990. The station at Tintern survives as a visitor centre, as do some of the railway bridges over the River Wye. The station at Monmouth Troy was dismantled and re-erected at Winchcombe on the heritage Gloucestershire Warwickshire Railway.

The line meandered alongside the River Wye, crossing between England and Wales for part of its route and passed through an undulating area famed for its beauty. Views would have included those of dense wooded hillsides, including parts of the Forest of Dean. If you continued north from Monmouth, towards Ross-on-Wye, the line snaked through the scenic gorge at Symonds Yat. Whilst on the section south from Monmouth, the train would have run past the romantic and extensive ruins of Tintern Abbey, before reaching the Severn Estuary. Part of the trackbed is used by the Wye Valley Walk.

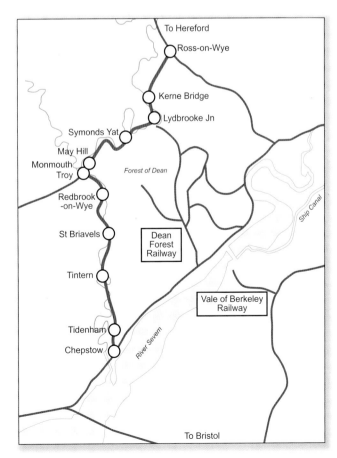

The valley of the River Wye was 'celebrated for its lofty cliffs, winding course and picturesque scenery' by Bradshaw. The GWR Monmouth–Chepstow line and the Wireworks link crossed the tidal reaches of the River Wye at Tintern. The river at Tintern, seen in October 2003, acts as the boundary between England and Wales here. *Author*

Tintern station sign in GWR black and white lettering pictured in October 2003. Even though the relatively large station was once busy with visitors to the nearby ruined and romantic remains of Tintern Abbey, it closed to passengers in January 1959. Today the station is a visitor centre. *Author*

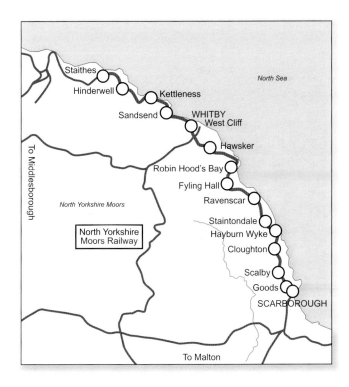

A poster promoting rail travel to the Yorkshire coast produced by the LNER. The view of the coast near Whitby, with precipitous cliffs and headlands, was painted by Frank Mason who spent time at sea. The coastal area was quoted by Bradshaw as 'scarcely to be exceeded for beauty in England'. The line here is now a footpath. *NRM/Science & Society Picture Library*

Robin Hood's Bay departures April 1956.

## The prospect of Whitby

The 21¾-mile Scarborough & Whitby Railway opened in 1885 and was operated by the NER from the outset. The single-line was winding and with some steep gradients. This led to the stalling of DMUs on a number of occasions when they were first introduced. The railway was not that busy in winter and never particularly profitable. A few economies were introduced in the 1950s and the line survived until March 1965.

The coastal route provided lovely views of headlands and bays, and ran through attractive and remote coastal settlements in the North York Moors, including the picturesque Robin Hood's Bay. At Whitby the railway crossed the tall 13 brick arches of the Larpool Viaduct over the River Esk, giving distant views of Whitby and the coast. The line then continued northward towards Saltburn and a number of other viaducts on this coastal section would also have given great views from the railway over the North Sea. Much of the former southern trackbed is used for the Scarborough to Whitby path and cycleway.

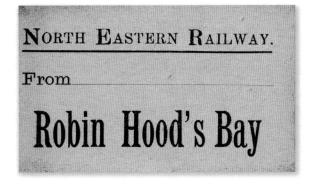

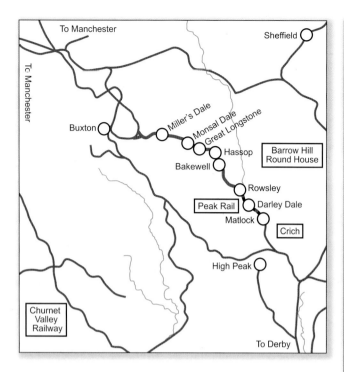

Monsal Dale in the Peak District National Park

# DERBYSHIRE

See Britain by Train    BRITISH RAILWAYS

## The Peak District

The railway through the Peak District was opened in sections and by 1863 became the 61-mile Derby–Manchester main line of the MR. Following the River Derwent before carving a route through the Derbyshire limestone hills, numerous tunnels were required, but at Haddon the tunnel was simply to conceal the railway from nearby Haddon Hall. Viaducts across Miller's Dale and Monsal Dale also had to be constructed. At the time of opening there was concern by some about damage to the scenic beauty of the area, but today the railway blends in well. The area has long been popular with tourists and the station at Monsal Dale was originally provided mainly for visitors to the area. Rowsley, for some years, also had 'for Chatsworth' added in timetables.

The main line was used by crack expresses and this railway was never even proposed for closure in the Beeching Report. Nonetheless, it was closed as a main through route in March 1967 and the 19-mile section between Great Rocks and Matlock, via Bakewell, was closed completely.

I travelled along this route, hauled by a Class 44 diesel, appropriately nicknamed 'Peaks'. Careering along over viaducts and through tunnels, past a beautiful area of the Peak District sometimes known as 'Little Switzerland' with its rugged and wooded scenery, stone walls and rocky limestone peaks, was a real joy. Part of the closed trackbed, including tunnels, has become the Monsal Trail, a scenic cycle and walkway, whilst part is used by Peak Rail, a heritage railway from Matlock to Rowsley that has plans to extend back to Bakewell.

LMR poster showing the spectacular Monsal Dale, in the Peak District, with a steam train crossing Monsal Viaduct. The artwork was by Peter Collins. Bradshaw described the area as 'one of the most enchanting districts in the world, unsurpassable in boldness, grandeur and magnificence'. *NRM/Science & Society Picture Library*

Miller's Dale departures April 1956.

**MILLER'S DALE** (Derby)
Miles 159¼. Map Sq. 12. Clos. day Tue.
From St. Pancras.
1st cl.—Single 37/8, Return 75/4.
3rd cl.—Single 25/1, Return 50/2.

| St. Pan. | Mill. D. | Mill. D. | St. Pan. |
|---|---|---|---|
| a.m. | | a.m. | |
| 4 15 | 9 2 | 8 13 | 11 33 |
| 8 15er | 12 15 | 10 5r | 2 1 |
| 8 15s | 12 15 | p.m. | |
| 10 15r | 1 42 | 12 39s | 4 33 |
| p.m. | | 2 49er | 6 14 |
| 2 15r | 5 39 | 2 49s | 6 19 |
| 4 15r | 7 56 | 4 55r | 8 38 |
| 6 40r | 10 16 | 6 55 | 10 55 |
| Sunday Trains. | | | |
| a.m. | | a.m. | |
| 8 30 | 1 9 | 10 5r | 3 0 |
| p.m. | | 10 42 | 3 25 |
| 12 30 | 5 44 | p.m. | |
| 3 30 | 7 46 | 3 5 | 7 20 |
| 6 10r | 10 9 | 3 45 | 8 50 |
| — | — | 7 4 | 11 30 |

e Not Saturday.
r Refreshment Car.
s Saturday only.

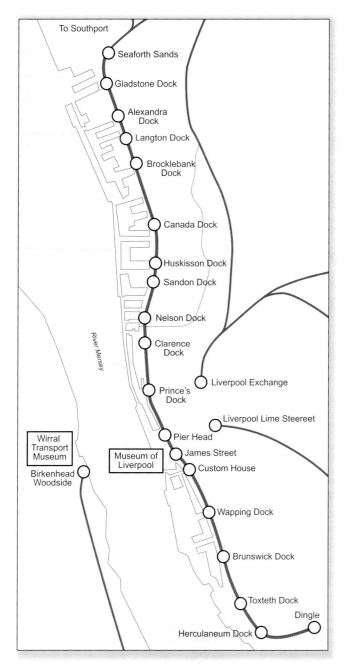

## The Overhead Railway

I add just one more line to the end of the list, as it is certainly not in the category of a countryside scenic line. The Liverpool Overhead Railway opened in 1893. It was to be the only overhead railway in the British Isles. After World War 2, the 6½-mile route was one of the few urban lines that escaped nationalisation in 1948. In the mid-1950s, areas of intensive corrosion were discovered on some sections of the elevated rolled iron deck plates. A study was undertaken to examine the extent of repairs required and it was realised that funds were insufficient for the £2 million estimated for this work. Efforts to persuade a takeover, or mount a rescue bid, were unsuccessful and, amidst massive protest, the line was closed in December 1956. As such, the LOR has been the only, very heavily-used and considerable stretch of electric urban railway to be lost in Britain. Little remains today and reopening is most unlikely.

Emerging from a tunnel at its southern end, the elevated line would have provided an uninterrupted view of the River Mersey, together with an urban landscape of industry, warehouses and docks, on one side and views of Liverpool's Anglican cathedral on the other. It would have passed behind the Royal Liver Building and Pier Head, before heading north through more docks bustling with stevedores, sailors and ships. Views of Birkenhead and the Wirral Peninsula would have been seen in the distance on the far side of the busy River Mersey.

Bradshaw described the docks at Liverpool as 'the grand lions of the town, extend in one magnificent range of 5 miles'. The Liverpool Overhead Railway would have had an ever-changing view over the high dock walls and city, but here the six-faced Victoria Tower or 'docker's clock' can still be seen from the former course of the railway in October 2006. *Author*

# 23
# Steaming back from scrap

The railways had used steam traction almost from the outset. Coal was plentiful and relatively cheap and locomotives gradually developed in size, efficiency and power. By the time the Big Four railways were established, they produced their own distinctive types of locomotives. They also competed with each other and, in 1938, LNER 'A4' Pacific *Mallard* reached 126mph, a world record. This said, the locomotives of the other railways were equally impressive such as the powerful GWR 'King' class, the LMS streamlined 'Princess Coronation' class and the SR's innovative 'Merchant Navy' class.

**PINES EXPRESS**

LMS Royal Scot class 4-6-0 No 6115 *Scots Guardsman*. Built in Glasgow in 1927, it starred in the film 'Night Mail' and was withdrawn in 1966. Although two of the 70 original locomotives were saved from being scrapped, No 6115 is seen here in a state of disrepair at Tyseley Locomotive Works in July 2001. The locomotive was subsequently restored to full working order, until again requiring an overhaul in 2017. *Author*

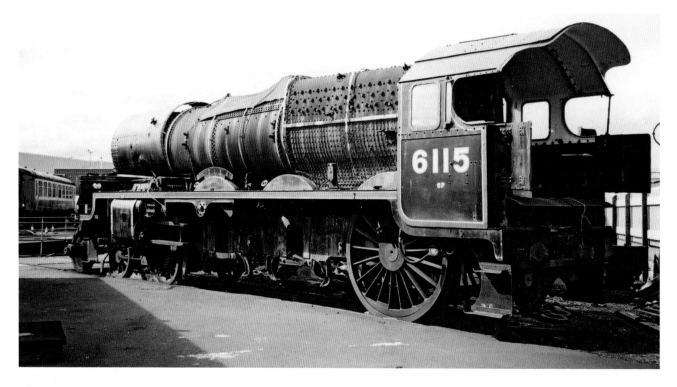

No 45699 *Galatea*, the LMS 'Jubilee' class 4-6-0, is seen on the heritage Mid-Norfolk Railway in June 2014. The locomotive was withdrawn in 1964 and sent to Barry scrapyard. It was rescued in 1980. Whilst perhaps the location and BR maroon livery might not be quite historically perfect for this locomotive, it is equally all about the magic of live steam and having fun. *A. Axcell*

The main section of the ex-GCR closed in May 1969. Today the Great Central Railway heritage line is the only double-track preserved main line. Here Ivatt Class 2 2-6-0 No 46521, saved from Barry scrapyard, conveys a rake of BR Mark 1 'Blood and Custard' carriages, in April 2015. This coach livery was gradually replaced by a maroon livery, together with regional variations, from 1956. *A. Axcell*

Although there were main line celebrities, in general BR inherited a huge collection of about 20,000 locomotives of all sizes, colour, power and design; countless were in poor condition after intensive use during World War 2. However, unlike many European railways that moved to electrification after World War 2, BR continued with the development of steam and the BR Standard classes of locomotives were built. This decision was taken because steam technology was widespread at the time and they were cheaper to build than diesel or electric locomotives. A further economic factor was that Britain had huge coal reserves and would not have to import so much oil.

BR built 2,537 new steam locomotives in the period up to 1960 when *Evening Star* was the last locomotive to be built at Swindon Works. Of the Standard designs, 999 were built in varying sizes and power to cover all types of traffic. They were a far cry from the earlier locomotives and incorporated all the best features from the pre-Grouping locomotives; working parts were mostly straightforward to access, they were easier to maintain and generally more efficient.

Then it was somewhat abruptly recognised that steam traction looked outdated, oil prices had fallen, whilst employing skilled workers for the arduous and dirty work of driving a steam locomotive became increasingly difficult. BR was losing money and it increasingly looked like an outdated organisation. It wanted to modernise its image and turn quickly from steam to diesel and electric traction.

LMS 'Black 5', 4-6-0 No 45379 dating from 1937, was withdrawn in 1965 and sent to Barry scrapyard, before being rescued in 1974. It is seen in July 2016 from the author's garden at Four Marks. This class of locomotive, introduced in 1934 by William Stanier, was most successful and survived until the end of steam on BR. Several examples of this class escaped the scrapyard. *Author*

SR 'West Country' 'air smoothed' Light Pacific 4-6-2 No 34007 *Wadebridge* was designed by Oliver Bulleid. Withdrawn from service in 1965, it was also saved from Barry scrapyard and purchased for preservation in 1981. It is photographed at Medstead & Four Marks station in March 2016, before being withdrawn for a heavy overhaul. *A. Axcell*

SR rebuilt 'Battle of Britain' Pacific 4-6-2 No 34059 *Sir Archibald Sinclair* on the heritage Bluebell Railway in September 2010. The original cab gauges had ultraviolet lights so that they could be read, but would not distract night-time driving. The locomotive was rescued from Barry scrapyard and is one of many that are preserved over 50 years since the end of Southern Region steam in 1967. *Author*

Consequently, steam engines were rapidly withdrawn, even the *Flying Scotsman* would have been scrapped had not Alan Pegler stepped in to buy it. Many of the BR Standard classes were almost new and had years of future use ahead, but a great steam tradition was quickly swept away. The last BR standard-gauge steam passenger service ran in August 1968; huge crowds lined the tracks between Liverpool, Manchester and Carlisle to witness the event. Even then it was not quite the end of the line for regular coal-fired steam trains. Steam locomotives were used for freight in Northern Ireland until 1970 and on London Transport for works trains and shunting duties until 1971. Steam continued to be used on NCB lines until the early 1980s.

Every BR locomotive had been allocated to, or based at, one of the network of over 600 engine sheds that once dotted the network. Each shed was given a number from 1A at Willesden to 89A at Oswestry. The end of steam resulted in the inevitable closure of these steam sheds. A number had been bombed and damaged during the war. BR had been slow to repair some of these and the end of steam was often accompanied by a period of dereliction at many of the sheds.

The open fire box of 4-4-0 No 925 *Cheltenham*, a member of the 'Schools' class as they became known. They were designed by Richard Maunsell for the Southern Railway and named after public schools. The locomotive is part of the National Collection and is seen on the heritage Watercress Line heading up the bank from Alton on a wet July day in 2015. *Author*

The engine sheds were of three main types: the roundhouse based around a turntable, the straight road shed accessible from either end and a dead end shed accessible from only one end. A number of early roundhouses have long been closed, such as those at Derby, Leeds and Camden, simply because the central turntable became too small for the increasing size of locomotives. Whilst these older roundhouses have survived and are treasures, later roundhouses were less fortunate and have been demolished. Exceptions include the closed St Blazey engine shed at Par, laid out in an arc and facing a working turntable, along with the heritage Barrow Hill, which is the last surviving working roundhouse.

As for the straight road engine shed, a number of heritage examples still house steam locomotives. They include Didcot 81E, once allocated almost 50 locomotives, Carnforth 24L, once allocated over 40 locomotives, Tunbridge Wells West 75F, once allocated about 25 locomotives and Aberdeen Ferryhill 61B once allocated about 40 locomotives. Many closed engine sheds still survive in new roles long after their railway use ended. These range from small sheds such as at Moretonhampstead, originally allocated a single locomotive, to larger ones such as Hull Dairycoats that was once allocated 145 locomotives.

Some steam sheds were converted for diesel use, but the conversion to diesel traction was not without its problems. A number of early diesel locomotives proved not to be very reliable or powerful, resulting in some diesel classes being withdrawn very early on.

In contrast, the introduction of DMUs on branch lines was effective and reduced costs, although many were introduced too late and without other economies to save branch and secondary lines.

In 1962 BR employed about 60,000 men in 29 railway works. The ever-reducing railway network, the rapid demise of steam and the greater efficiency of diesel engines was to diminish activity in the workshops. Many former locomotive works closed, including those at Ashford, Brighton, Darlington, Horwich, Gorton, Stratford and Swindon. Track was torn up and numerous redundant buildings were demolished or put to new non-railway uses. The remaining railway works were privatised in 1989.

GWR No 6960 *Raveningham Hall* is a 4-6-0 'Modified Hall' class built in 1944 at Swindon. It was withdrawn in 1964 and later saved from Barry scrapyard in 1972. Note the large train reporting numbers on the front which allowed signallers to identify the train. The locomotive is seen on the heritage Great Central Railway, in April 2015. *A. Axcell*

On the right is GWR No 6998 *Burton Agnes Hall*, a 'Modified Hall' class, built at Swindon in 1949 and withdrawn by BR in 1966. On the left, the second GWR locomotive No 5322, is a 2-6-0 that was built in 1917 and originally sent to France as part of the war effort. Withdrawn by BR in 1964 both locomotives survived the cutters torch. They are seen resting at the Didcot Railway Centre in May 2013. *A. Axcell*

GWR 0-6-0PT No 6430 built at Swindon in 1937, with an autocoach recreating a GWR branch line atmosphere at North Weald on the heritage Epping Ongar Railway in June 2015. The autocoach, or push-pull train, could travel up and down branches without the need for the locomotive to run around the carriage. *A. Axcell*

A 'Pines Express' recreation makes a spirited start from Ropley in October 2016, headed by BR Standard Class 4MT 2-6-0 No 76017. The locomotive was withdrawn in 1965 and spent years languishing at Barry scrapyard before being rescued in 1974. It is seen leading BR Standard Class 9F 2-10-0 No 92212 which was also saved from scrap. *A. Axcell*

The rapid withdrawal of steam locomotives even caused congestion at some scrap yards. At Dai Woodham's Barry Scrapyard in South Wales in 1968 over 200 locomotives were just left to rust as there was so much other work in scrapping coal wagons. Fortunately, this allowed the preservation movement to gather pace and eventually save most of the rusting hulks for preservation. Without this particular scrapyard, the heritage railway movement would have been far worse off in providing steam traction today. In a twist of fate, some real treasures of steam locomotives, that had been destined for scrap, today run on heritage railways that had been destined for closure.

*Opposite top:* LNER 4-6-2 'A4' Pacific No 4464 *Bittern*, in Garter Blue LNER livery, in September 2014. Sir Nigel Gresley was the designer of these locomotives in the 1930s and *Bittern* was withdrawn from service by BR in the 1966. Several express steam locomotives, including the *Flying Scotsman*, can on occasion be seen working at slower speeds on heritage railways. *A. Axcell*

*Bottom:* Ordered by the LNER in 1928 and built by Beyer, Peacock and Company, Class B12/3 4-6-0 No 8572 in LNER apple-green livery departs from Horsted Keynes on the Bluebell Railway in October 2016. Based on the North Norfolk Railway, the exchange of locomotives between preserved railways is a feature of the modern preservation scene. *A. Axcell*

# 24
# Railway hotels and hospitality

The North Western Hotel at Liverpool was originally owned by the LNWR, opening in 1871. The huge symmetrical building adjoining the station was designed in a mixture of baronial hall and French chateau styles by Alfred Waterhouse. It ceased being used as a hotel in 1933, but when viewed here in April 2006 was used for student accommodation. *Author*

The railways pioneered the hotel industry in Britain and for 150 years ran some of the grandest hotels in the country. The first railway owned hotel was built at Euston in 1838. Over subsequent years numerous hotels were opened by the railways. Some were built as an integral part of the station, others had direct links to platforms, sometimes by passenger subways or covered ways. Equally a number were a distance away from the nearest station, requiring the railway to provide road transport.

When first built, railway hotels were frequently at the cutting edge of new technology and luxury. Respectable architects were commissioned and produced a variety of attractive buildings that have stood the test of time. At its peak there were about 120 railway owned hotels throughout Britain, once the largest hotel empire in the world.

The hotels were built in many different sizes, localities and styles, but eventually fell into three main categories: firstly, those used primarily for business in main towns and cities; secondly, hotels were provided for those using port shipping services; finally, as leisure time increased, those used primarily for pleasure, the country house hotel in attractive rural areas, often with golf facilities, or by the sea.

The LYR Exchange Hotel in Liverpool was opened in 1888 and rightly described in Baedeker's Guide as 'handsome'. Although the hotel closed in 1971 and the station closed in April 1977, the hotel frontage and clock were retained when the site was redeveloped for offices. The frontage is seen in April 2006. *Author*

Gradually a number of hotels had become increasingly outdated with their facilities, some having just one bathroom and toilet on each floor. As a consequence in the 1930s, closures began and there was a decline in the numbers of railway owned hotels. The LMS closed the North Western Hotel at Liverpool in 1933 and the Midland Grand at St Pancras in 1935. Both were huge imposing buildings and after closure were saved from demolition, with that at St Pancras reopening as a hotel in 2011.

The GWR in the 1930s disposed of hotels at Swindon and Bristol and abandoned plans for new hotels at Birmingham, Swansea and Looe. Yet at the same time extensions to Tregenna Castle Hotel at St Ives, the Manor House Hotel at Mortonhampstead and the Great Western Royal Hotel at Paddington were undertaken.

When the railways were nationalised in 1948, they took over almost 50 remaining railway hotels. The hotels at Cannon Street, Holborn Viaduct and London Bridge stations were all damaged beyond repair during World War 2. The requisition of the Lord Warden Hotel at Dover and the Cruden Bay Hotel in Scotland during the war also led to their closure. After the war, the Lord Warden Hotel became offices, whilst the Cruden Bay Hotel was demolished in 1952, as a new owner prepared to refurbish the hotel could not be found. The imposing building was in sharp contrast to a single-storey wooden railway hotel at Port Victoria in Kent which was also demolished in 1952.

The LSWR French Renaissance-styled South Western Hotel at Southampton was also used by those staying before they crossed the Atlantic. Some guests were booked on the ill-fated *Titanic*. The hotel closed in 1939 and was requisitioned for war service. It is now in residential use and is pictured in May 1995. *Author*

203

The SER City Terminus Hotel at Cannon Street opened in 1866 and had 84 bedrooms, but just five bathrooms. The hotel was damaged beyond repair during World War 2 and was subsequently demolished. The Italianate style reflected that of Charing Cross as both were designed by E. M. Barry. *Author's collection*

The ex-GNSR Cruden Bay Hotel had its own electric 3ft 6½-in gauge tram line from the branch line station. It was the most northerly electrified line in Britain. The tramway closed in 1940 and the hotel was demolished after being requisitioned during World War 2. A preserved tram is seen at the Grampian Transport Museum at Alford in 2011. *Courtesy Grampian Transport Museum*

The Euston Hotel, the first ever, survived the Blitz of World War 2 only to be torn down by BR in 1963. Others were being sold off at this time, but by 1970 British Transport Hotels still owned 32 hotels, providing over 6,000 beds, the fourth largest hotel chain in the country. Although a new railway hotel was built in St Andrews in 1968, this proved to be the last and the final railway owned hotel was sold off in 1983.

A significant number of former railway owned hotel buildings have survived under private ownership, in some form or other. Several that are still open have changed their names, whilst a number have been pulled down. Those demolished, not mentioned above, include the railway hotels at Bath, Birmingham, Bletchley, Colchester, Dorking, Eastleigh, Glasgow St Enoch, Grimsby, Holyhead, Hunstanton, Lincoln, Neyland, Normanton and St Neots.

The smaller and sometimes humbler privately-owned railway hotel, inn or hostelry adjoining stations have also contracted with the loss of stations. In many cases after the closure of a line, the only sign of a former station was the nearby aptly named station or railway hotel, although many have also since changed their names, been put to new uses or redeveloped. Furthermore, all the inns and public houses that were once owned by the railways have long been disposed of.

The ex-GER Felix Hotel at Felixstowe opened in 1903. Wallis Simpson, whose intended marriage to King Edward VIII brought about his abdication, was one of the hotel guests in the 1930s. Closure came in 1951 and the hotel was put up for sale. The imposing cliff top building is pictured in August 1994 and is now in residential use. *Author*

The Station Hotel at Framlingham is a typical hostelry adjoining a railway station and is viewed in June 2012. The building was constructed with the station in 1859. The station itself closed to passengers in November 1952 and to freight in April 1965, but almost all of the railway buildings remain and the hotel is still open. *Author*

It is still possible to sample the pleasures of many former railway hotels. Some great treasures remain in use throughout Britain. In Scotland, Gleneagles is a well-known former railway hotel. In addition to its golf course it once had a long siding to the rear of the hotel to provide coal and provisions, whilst its station still remains open. Also in Scotland, the former NBR Hotel in Edinburgh is one of the most striking features of that city, whilst the nearby Caledonian Hotel has stained glass crests of towns no longer served by the railway. The Adelphi Hotel in Liverpool has MR monogramed bedroom ceilings and the Midland Hotel in Manchester has a golden Wyvern. Huge GWR initials are set into the entrance of the hotel at Paddington and the LMS crest is to be found at the Queens Hotel at Leeds.

The Station Inn at Holbeach adjoined the M&GN station. Offering a room for the night, a landlord was once my great grandfather, Harry Clark. The buildings and well-illustrated pub sign, seen in August 1994, were demolished in 2014, having survived many years after the station closed to passengers in February 1959. *Author*

The Captain Fryatt public house at Parkeston, seen in August 1994, named after the intrepid GER ship's captain who attempted to ram a German submarine during World War 1. He was captured and shot without a fair trial. After the war, his body was returned to England and given a funeral at St Paul's Cathedral. The hostelry remains open. *Author*

The Adelphi Midland Hotel at Liverpool, with detailing of the monogrammed stonework showing 'AM' crowned with a Liver Bird, seen in June 2007. The hotel once catered for passengers before they crossed the Atlantic to America. The hotel was rebuilt in its current form by the MR just before World War 1. It is still in use and retains several of its original features. *Author*

The former railway hotels at Turnberry, Moretonhampstead, Fleetwood, Rudyard Lake, Keswick, Dornock and Strathpeffer all remain open, long after their nearby stations closed. Elsewhere a number of ex-railway hotels retain their direct passageways to stations and in London the St Pancras Hotel has turned the original station booking hall into a bar.

There were also other forms of hospitality on lines and stations that have closed. Almost all of the large urban stations that have closed had refreshment facilities. Tea rooms, sometimes with licences to sell alcohol, were also a welcome addition to tourist stations such as Ballater and Callander in Scotland and Corwen in Wales. In England Hunstanton and Ripon had refreshment rooms, together with those at Ventnor and Ilfracombe.

Restaurant cars, unlike railway hotels and refreshment rooms, have all but disappeared. They first ran in 1879 and were a cherished feature of railways for many years. At one time, there were about 200 daily restaurant cars on the LNER and in 1927 the LMS alone served 10,000 partridge and 500 tonnes of fish in its restaurant cars; clearly they were a popular feature that encouraged railway travel.

The Gleneagles Hotel is one of the most famous former Scottish railway hotels, with its own golf course. Opened in 1924, the nearby Crieff Junction station was renamed Gleneagles to help promote the hotel and the station is seen in October 2011. The hotel and station remain open, but the branch to Crieff, on the left-hand side of the platform, closed in July 1964. *Author*

I had some criticism of BR in the Beeching era, but there were about 150 restaurant cars in daily service towards the end of the British Rail era in 1994. This long established and well-loved passenger facility has gradually been withdrawn since privatisation and the prize-winning restaurant cars on the London–Norwich line were removed, after over 100 years of service, in 2008. On today's railways, although meals are served at first class seats on some long-distance services, there was in 2017 just one traditional restaurant car service left, on the GWR.

Ballater station with Queen Victoria's private lavatory, which was built to designs approved by the monarch, seen in June 2009. Victoria and subsequent royalty used the station before closure in February 1966. Sadly, fire destroyed much of the building in May 2015, but rebuilding of the mainly wooden station is underway. *Author*

# 25
# Time travellers

Some lines that were proposed for closure in the Beeching Report were reprieved, the Heart of Wales Line being a lengthy rural example saved from closure because it crossed marginal constituencies. This was not the case for other, far busier lines that could be closed without serious political consequences. Vigorous protest about hardship saved a few lines. Wider social and economic considerations began to lead to fewer closures, but the fuel crisis of 1974 made it plain that without railways the country could grind to a halt. After this event closures were few and far between.

Fortunately, since the dark days of the Beeching cuts, attempts have been made to restore some of the closures, both by reopening individual stations and lines. In Scotland, they have reopened lines to passengers such as those to Alloa, Bathgate and others in and around Glasgow. The Hilton Junction–Ladybank line and the northern section of the Waverley Route have also returned as part of the national passenger network. In South Wales the lines to Aberdare, Ebbw Vale and the Barry–Bridgend–Maesteg routes have all been reopened.

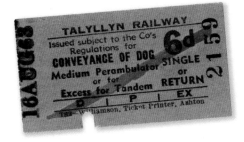

In 1951 the Talyllyn Railway in Wales became the world's first preserved line. *Sir Haydn*, originally built for the Corris Railway in 1878, is preparing to leave Tywyn in June 1999 with a collection of historic carriages, providing a unique travel experience from the past. The success of the Talyllyn was followed by the Ffestiniog and a number of other narrow-gauge lines have been reopened. *Author*

The Bluebell Railway in East Sussex was one of the first standard-gauge heritage lines, opening in 1960, after the line had closed two years earlier. SECR-preserved 'H' class 0-4-4T No 263, dating from 1905, is seen at Sheffield Park in March 2013 and helps give the line a Victorian atmosphere. *A. Axcell*

In England, Mansfield has a population of over 100,000 and after closure was the largest town not served by a railway, but had its line reopened. Peterborough–Spalding, Barnsley–Penistone, Walsall–Rugeley, Nuneaton–Coventry–Leamington Spa, Eastleigh–Romsey and the Oxford–Bicester routes have all reopened to passengers. Links to Corby, Heysham and Birmingham Snow Hill have also been restored, together with a number of other useful connections in London.

The Ravenglass & Eskdale Railway in the Lake District was converted from a closed narrow-gauge railway into a miniature line, and is one of a number operating in the country. *River Esk*, dating from 1923, is seen storming up the line in September 1999. The outsized bridge is a reminder that the railway was originally built as a 3ft narrow-gauge line opening in 1875. *Author*

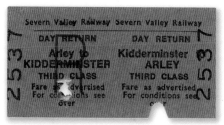

The Kidderminster–Bridgnorth line closed to passengers in September 1963, but was eventually reopened by the Severn Valley Railway. The 16-mile heritage railway hosts many main line locomotives. A train hauled by Ivatt 2-6-0 Class 2 No 46521 is pulling away from Arley, a GWR country station with its oil lamps and well-kept station gardens, in August 1992. *Author*

The cost of reopening lines in Britain also seems to have become ridiculously high-priced. In some cases, figures that seem almost 20 times more expensive than those in Europe have been put forward. The figures appear to be as suspect as those in the Beeching Report, but then they do say that history repeats itself.

Equally there remains a long list of lines that should be reopened. I simply offer nothing more than my personal short list of just 10 or so lost lines that could in pragmatic terms have their routes safeguarded from any future non-railway development and eventually be reopened. I recognise that this very short list excludes a number of equally important closed railways, where a

real effort is being made to reopen the line and that some will quibble with my selection. The list was based on the busy usage of a number of lines before closure, whilst some routes were not even proposed for closure by Dr Beeching, others would provide greater flexibility to the existing railway network. As such, I hope there would be agreement that many lines on the list are deserving contenders to be reopened.

- Oxford–Cambridge: the route could form part of an outer orbital railway for London.
- Lewes–Uckfield would also provide flexibility for the congested Brighton line.
- Waverley route completion will complement the success of the northern section.
- Bere Alston–Tavistock–Okehampton would be a resilient alternative to the coast line.
- Stourbridge–Walsall–Litchfield, with part as an extension of the Midland Metro.
- Ashington, Blyth and Washington as part of an extended Tyne & Wear Metro.
- Skipton–Colne would reinstate a trans-Pennine route and help with regeneration.
- A spur into Skelmersdale, a large town in the North West without a station.
- Bristol–Portishead would provide traffic relief in a growing area.
- Either a link to Levenmouth, or St Andrews, or Wisbech, or Coalville.

Where lines have closed, a growing number are being used as recreational footpaths and cycleways. The first Sustrans traffic-free cycling route was opened in the late 1970s and numerous local authorities, landowners and others have come together to expand this network. The cycleways and long-distance paths can also form significant wildlife corridors and in this respect lost railways continue to serve an important function.

Several lines that have been closed have reopened as heritage railways. There are many of great distinction and about 500 miles of heritage line. This includes a number of lines that are 10 or more miles in length such as the Bluebell, Churnet Valley, East Lancashire, Gloucestershire Warwickshire, Great Central, Keith & Dufftown, Kent & East Sussex, Llangollen, Mid-Hants, Mid-Norfolk, North Yorkshire Moors, Severn Valley, Strathspey, Swanage, Weardale, Wensleydale and West Somerset railways.

'Black 5' 4-6-0 No 45305 on the named train 'The South Yorkshireman'. The original Bradford–Marylebone express ran via Sheffield Victoria and over the ex-GCR main line. Today it is recreated as a dining train on the preserved double-track section of the GCR heritage line and is seen here in April 2015. *A. Axcell*

Moreover, the narrow-gauge Ffestiniog & Welsh Highland Railways have well over 10 miles of track. A number of new narrow and miniature-gauge tourist lines have also been constructed on closed sections of standard-gauge trackbeds. Extension of the Corris Railway and reopening of part of the Glyn Valley Tramway are just some of the narrow-gauge projects under active consideration. The iconic Lynton & Barnstaple Railway is a certainty for expansion in the future.

Many standard-gauge heritage railways are also planning, or already working on, exciting route extensions, some of which involve difficult issues. Heritage railways are continually expanding and few lines ever consider themselves complete. Extensions to heritage railways restore public transport, whilst providing wider social and economic benefits to the areas served. Yet quite often short-sighted and ad hoc new developments have been built on disused railway lines, even on those connected to existing heritage routes. In some cases, these new developments have seriously compromised further expansion plans.

In Wales the Barmouth Junction/Morfa Mawddach–Ruabon line ran through Llangollen, but closed to remaining freight traffic in April 1968. The GWR station, viewed in September 2003, became the centre for the heritage Llangollen Railway. Situated in the Dee Valley, services run between Llangollen and Corwen. *Author*

*Above:* In Scotland, the heritage Bo'ness & Kinneil Railway also has a large exhibition area with railway stock collected from all over Scotland. The branch once saw coal traffic to the port of Bo'ness on the Firth of Forth. A train hauled by an 0-6-0T, No 17 *Braeriach*, celebrating 50 years of the Scottish Railway Preservation Society, leaves Bo'ness station in June 2011. *Author*

Ivatt class 2 2-6-0 No 46521 arrived at Barry scrapyard in 1967. Saved from scrap, the locomotive has worked on several heritage railways and is seen on the Nene Valley Railway at Wansford in September 2016. The Jacobean-styled local stone station building in the background dates from the opening of the line in 1845. *A. Axcell*

BR Standard Class 9F 2-10-0 No 92212. These powerful engines were rapidly withdrawn when dieselisation was introduced. The locomotive, seen taking water at Ropley in February 2016, was built in 1959 and withdrawn by BR after only about eight years of service, some of which was spent on the S&D. Several of the class were saved from scrap. *A. Axcell*

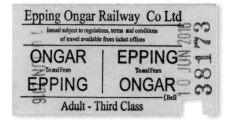

BR embarked on an extensive dieselisation programme. Class 37 diesel-electric locomotive built in 1961 and restored as D6729, in BR green livery, is seen in August 2012 at North Weald on the heritage Epping Ongar Railway. A typical GER station building is to be noted behind the locomotive on this branch, which was for a period part of the LT network. *A. Axcell*

DMUs were provided for many branch lines, but a Derby-built lightweight battery electric multiple-unit was used on the Aberdeen–Ballater route from 1958. This surviving two-car set is seen at Milton of Crathes on the heritage Royal Deeside Railway in June 2016. The unit was withdrawn from passenger service in 1966 and after departmental use was subsequently preserved. *Dr A. Grundy*

The Hampshire Units were one of a number of classes of DEMUs introduced by the Southern Region. The unit, seen here heading west from Alton in July 2015, was used on the last Alton–Winchester service in February 1973. Built in 1959 it now operates on the heritage Watercress Line that has reopened the Alton–Alresford section of the route. *Author*

Red fire buckets, in this case painted with S&D initials, at Washford on the heritage West Somerset Railway in June 2009. Water-filled buckets were widespread in the days of steam and before fire extinguishers were in general use. The S&D closed in March 1966, but being such an evocative railway, preservation of sections of the old route are underway. *Author*

Looking to the future, it is likely that more and more lost lines will reopen either as heritage routes, or as part of the national network. Consequently, central and local government need to work together towards implementing much stronger safeguards for disused railways, with the aim to prevent any fully obstructing other types of development. This should include sections of lost line that currently appear to offer little prospect of reopening, but that may well have a long-term potential for future railway reuse.

Finally, history has shown that no railway line, or railway building, is ever really safe. Yet the total number of rail journeys on the national network across Britain has more than doubled in the last 20 years, and demand for rail travel, away from increasingly congested and polluting roads, has been on an upward trend. History has shown when passenger numbers fall railway lines are closed; when numbers rise surely then even more railway lines should be re-opened.

Didcot Railway Centre is one of many great living railway heritage centres. The museum uses the GWR 1932 locomotive shed, whilst a large collection of GWR engines, stock and historic railway equipment are on display. A crossing lamp at Didcot, seen in June 1993, survives, but coal trains to the distant power station are no more. *Author*

# Index

## Further reading by this author

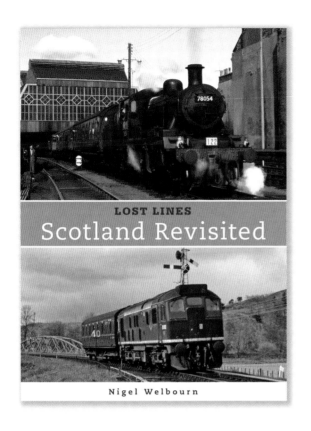

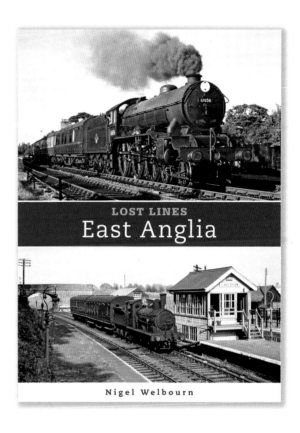

## Lost Lines: Scotland Revisited

### Nigel Welbourn

Nigel Welbourn heads north for a second exploration of the many interesting closed railways of Scotland. While lost lines in Scotland are often found in the romantically picturesque countryside, many others are to be discovered in the midst of highly industrialised locations, providing an unparalleled diversity of lines and traffic.

ISBN: 978 0 7110 3517 1

Price: £18

## Lost Lines: East Anglia

### Nigel Welbourn

After the infamous Beeching report of 1963 Nigel Welbourn recognised that irrevocable change was on the way, and began recording the railways of East Anglia for over 50 years. This book examines the decline culminating in closure, which has left huge rural areas of East Anglia without any railway services, but equally providing a fascinating legacy of lost railway remains.

ISBN: 978 0 7110 3748 9

Price: £18

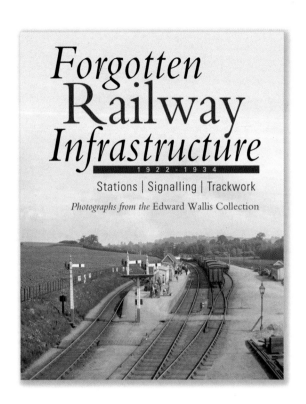

# Forgotten Railway Infrastructure

## E Wallis

This is the fourth book in the hugely successful series of 'Southern' and Great Western' Infrastructure images from the camera of the late Edward Wallis. Rather than concentrating on a specific railway company, this selection is more widespread and includes the LNWR, its successor the LMS and the LNER as well as a number of smaller concerns such as the Stratford & Midland Junction Railway.

Edward Wallis was a signal engineer working for the Southern Railway in the 1920s until his untimely demise in the mid-1930s. During that period he travelled the length and breadth of England recording signalling and track work scenes. He pointed his camera at the track, stations, and signals, in so doing providing what is probably a unique perspective on railway life in the 1920s and early 1930s. Nearly all of the collection is also previously unseen, having lain in drawers of glass negatives until copied now for the first time.

His legacy is an archive of incredible views primarily of the Southern Railway but also feature the Great Western and to a lesser extent the other companies. The SR and GWR have already been presented in respective volumes but now for the first time come examples from the other companies as well as a few SR/GWR that 'escaped' last time!

ISBN: 978 1909328723
Price: £14.95